MW01046110

WHAT HOSPITAL LEADERS ARE SAYING ABOUT "THE MISSION-DRIVEN HOSPITAL..."

"A compelling message to hospital leaders looking to breathe life into their organization's mission statement and make their hospital truly mission-driven. Bart provides a practical guide – and powerful analysis - that effectively demonstrates the crucial elements needed to align the mission with a hospital's performance."

BOB HOULDEN
Director, Educational Services & Governance Programs
Ontario Hospital Association

• • •

"Dr. Bart makes a compelling case for the importance of Mission statements in the best healthcare environments and then provides his detailed 5-C Mission model methodology for creating one and bringing it fully to life. Terrific material for all Boards and senior management teams."

TIMO HYTONEN
Former Vice President, Human Resources
Hospital for Sick Children (Toronto, Canada)
Senior Vice-President, Human Resources & Corporate Initiatives
Empire Life

• • •

"Bart has done an excellent job of capturing the essence of the importance of not only creating a Mission Statement, but also linking it to how one fundamentally focuses and aligns an organization. This book will assist hospital Executives by arming them with the ready answers as to how to respond to the many skeptics that refuse to embrace the need to invest valuable time in creating a Mission Statement."

MURRAY MARTIN
CEO,
Hamilton Health Sciences

• • •

"Bart's 5-C Mission Model provides a user friendly, easily understandable and highly implementable step-by-step recipe for success for every hospital in the country. It is a book that must be read by every healthcare leader. I loved it!"

DONNA CRIPPS
CEO,
Hamilton Niagara Haldimand Brant Local Health
Integration Network (LHIN)

• • •

"Very timely, informative, thought provoking and practical information for any NFP hospital or, for that matter, *any* healthcare organization particularly in these turbulent and potentially disruptive times. Excellent guidance based on groundbreaking peer hospital survey responses and Chris's extensive subject matter expertise."

MURRAY KILFOYLE, C.A., C.DIR.
Vice Chair,
St. Boniface Hospital

• • •

"Bart's book is written for hospital leaders but *relevant to all organizations within the broader healthcare sector.* If you are ready to embark on developing or renewing your strategic plan – Bart's book will provide you with the step-by-step and readily applied guidance to develop a winning mission for your organization. In fact, Dr. Bart's book recently helped me to lead my own team through an effective strategic planning renewal process which will make us truly become mission-driven.

Bart's book is a must read for Board members and Senior Leaders in order to understand the fundamental need and ultimate success in being *mission-driven* and the steps required to get there. His book will be my go-to tool for future inspiration and guidance whenever I question the level of mission-driven commitment in my organization."

LORRI LOWE, CMA, FCMA, C.DIR.
Executive Director
Maitland Valley Family Health Team

• • •

"Many hospital's mission statements become fixtures on the wall beside strategic planning documents of the past, lacking relevance and meaning for staff, stakeholders, and the communities that we serve. The Mission-Driven Hospital book and its 5-C Model is a must read for hospital executives looking to bring their organization's mission to life with inspiration and relevance every day across the organization, from the Board of Directors to our patients' bedsides."

ERIC VANDEWALL
President & CEO
Joseph Brant Memorial Hospital

• • •

"Chris Bart has waded into the complex world of hospitals and the healthcare environment and has brought clarity to the potential of the mission-driven hospital. Whether it's high tech, high touch, teaching, or community health that drives a hospital, the right mission statement has the power to guide it in best serving those in need of its services."

MIKE DEGAGNE
President, Nipissing University
Former Executive Director, Aboriginal Healing Foundation
Past Chairman, Queensway Carleton Hospital Board Director,
Champlain Local Health Integration Network

• • •

"I've been working in both private and public healthcare for most of my career. Chris Bart lays out an inspiring call to action and path to becoming a mission-driven healthcare organization. An important read!"

TREVOR FEDYNA
VP Business Development & COO,
Orion Health Services

• • •

"This book should be on every hospital board's and senior management team's "must read" list as they embark on their hospital strategic plan. It is an excellent resource with the potential to have a positive lasting impact in the healthcare sector.

With one "ah ha" moment after another, this book is exciting and inspirational. The reader wants to get right to work analyzing and improving their own hospital mission statement. Through the use of real life examples and referencing his own very extensive research, Dr. Bart has created a tool that will serve hospitals well into the future.

Moreover, in this time of increasing pressure on hospitals to do more with less, Dr. Bart has identified a "secret of success" that

impacts hospitals at all levels – from the CEO to the front line workers. He takes his readers through a logical and easy to follow "5-C
Mission Model" to improve hospital performance through the use of
a well crafted and properly implemented mission statement."

BARBARA LESLIE, DVM, MSc, CAE, C.Dir.
Vice Chair,
North Wellington Health Care Corporation

• • •

"I found Chris Bart's book to be an easy read but more importantly
informative, applicable and valuable…I think his 5-C Mission
Model is spot on."

SUE DENOMY
President/CEO,
Bluewater Health

• • •

"Chris Bart's book clearly represents what hospitals and hospital systems should do (but don't). The strategic planning cycle is short
and the strategic plan is usually not mission-driven. Thus there is a
significant gap here that Bart has identified and which is critical to
close in our sector. "

ERIC FONBERG MD MPH MBA CCFP(EM) C.Dir.
Chief of Staff
MacKenzie Health

• • •

"I want every one of my employees to read this book. It is a must
read for Directors at anytime, but particularly in advance of strategic
planning discussions. Bart's book is the perfect "how to do it and
why" that I have ever read. While talk of being mission-driven has
been around for years, Bart's book, ironically, is a pioneering work
on the subject. It is approachable, methodical, highly supported,

and eloquently written. It will save you years of aimlessly wandering through the wilderness of searching for what it means to be a mission-driven hospital."

DAVID MONTGOMERY, CA, CHE, CHRP, C.Dir.
President and CEO
Haldimand War Memorial Hospital and Edgewater Gardens

• • •

"This is a practical and inspiring book. Chris Bart's message is clear: "mission-driven" hospitals outperform other health care providers on virtually every measure. He has written a practical step-by-step guide that carefully explains how hospitals can make their mission the heart of all that they do, and why this is so essential. This book should be mandatory reading for every CEO and Board Chair in the Canadian health sector today.

We all understand the need for mission statements, but seldom think about the process of creating and communicating them. And yet, as Chris Bart explains in this inspiring book, careful creation, communication and coordination are key to the transformation of hospitals into high achieving "mission-driven" organizations. Bart's 5-C Mission Model is a step-by-step prescription for sustained long term success. Moreover, Bart's new book is a wake-up call for any hospital administrator who still believes a mission statement belongs only in the annual report and on the board room wall. The research underpinning Chris Bart's new book provides clear proof that the most successful hospitals are the ones that make their mission the heart of all they do. His 5-C Mission Model is a useful tool for any hospital embarking on strategic renewal."

DEREK NICE
Past Chair
Campbellford Memorial Hospital

• • •

"I found Bart's book to be a good read, fast paced and provocative; this book would serve as a thought provoking and excellent resource for hospital Board Chairs and Members alike. An enjoyable, and educational read!"

• • •

"I found Bart's book very enlightening. Dr. Bart looks at the mission statement from conception to integration and control....Like all good doctors, he examines the cause and not just the symptoms to develop the cure!"

• • •

"Planning a strategic planning process? Read "The Mission-Driven Hospital" first! Bart delivers a roadmap that will turn your mission statement into a powerful tool that meaningfully drives performance, engages your staff and community, and supports strategy deployment."

• • •

THE Mission-Driven HOSPITAL

TURNING NOBLE
ASPIRATIONS
INTO ACCOUNTABILITY
& ACTION!

Dr. Chris Bart, FCPA

*The world's leading authority
on organizational mission statements*

CORPORATE MISSIONS, INC.

Dr. Chris Bart, FCPA

Corporate Missions Inc.

1063 King Street West, Suite 230

Hamilton, ON Canada L8S 4S3

905-308-8455

chrisbart@corporatemissionsinc.com

www.corporatemissionsinc.com

ISBN: 978-0-9732247-8-8

Design and composition by John Reinhardt Book Design

For Patsy & David with love!

CONTENTS

The Mission-Driven Hospital

Why this book was written and
why *EVERY* Hospital Board Chair
and CEO must read it!!

THE IMPETUS FOR THIS BOOK has its roots in a *conundrum* most hospital CEOs and Board Chairs will readily recognize.

Let me explain.

Almost every hospital in the world has a mission statement. Why? Because mission statements are considered so important that the existence (and quality) of one is typically a key component of the evaluation criteria used during a hospital's formal accreditation (or re-accreditation) process. But hospitals are not alone in recognizing the value of the mission statement as a vital management tool. According to Bain and Company in its annual survey of 'management tools' in use by leading companies around the globe, the mission statement is used by 80 percent of the organizations surveyed and has earned the No. 1 spot on several occasions. Not surprisingly, many management experts and consultants today view an organization's mission statement as *the cornerstone* of, or starting point for, any strategic planning exercise.

There are many reasons to explain the popularity of this tool among hospitals.

By definition, mission statements are supposed to *guide and better focus* a hospital's actions to achieve its specific goals. They spell out the purposes for which hospitals exist. And, as I will show, if properly formulated and implemented, they serve as *an inspirational social contract* with each of a hospital's important *stakeholders*. Nowhere could these benefits be of more relevance than in the healthcare sector, particularly in our current era of "managed health," a time in which hospital budgets have become more and more restricted while tough new mandates and regulations have been imposed. In such an environment, a good mission statement can help set hospitals on the road to both more *wisely allocate their increasingly scarce resources* and to help ensure their survival. So it's no wonder hospitals worldwide have recognized the need to create and embrace the notion of a mission statement for their organizations.

Yet, here's where the conundrum kicks in.

Despite their widespread use, mission statements remain one of the least understood, least respected and most despised management tools in the world among workers and managers at all levels (even, surprisingly often, in the executive suite). For example: If you were to ask almost any employee, particularly at the front line, what the mission of their hospital was, you would likely get one of two responses: you'd either be met with a blank stare or a puzzled look; or you'd hear, "Oh, that (pause)...nonsense!" Indeed, the subject is one of the most frequently mentioned—and skewered—topics in the irreverent comic strip, Dilbert.

So what's the solution to the conundrum? How do you bring the respect that most intelligent, well-educated executives say they have for mission statements to all the stakeholders within—and associated with—the hospital? And how do you make its value seem real (and useful) to your workforce so it is embraced by each employee, thus improving individual performance and, as a direct result, helping to drive better hospital performance?

As a Professor of Strategy and Governance at the DeGroote School of Business at McMaster University in Hamilton, Ontario, I have been studying and writing about the use, misuse and value of mission statements for over ten years. One major conclusion that my research has confirmed over and over again is that there is a tremendous performance advantage to be obtained by those hospitals that sincerely *choose* to become what I call **mission-driven**.

By mission-driven, I mean that **every decision, action and behavior your hospital takes is rooted and linked to the aspirations, intentions, goals and objectives** *embedded in the mission*. But for this to happen, it means that *every* **person in your hospital knows, understands, appreciates and remembers the mission and most importantly, personally commits to carrying out the mission as it applies to his or her particular job.**

When everyone in your hospital has this understanding (and is confident that everyone else does, too) the *conundrum* vanishes and an almost magical transformation occurs. I call that metamorphosis *the mission mystique*—and it takes place because now there is no ambiguity. Everyone is reading from the same program. And everyone knows that they are acting in concert with a well-coordinated and focused group of individuals. Becoming mission-driven, however, is not something that will occur automatically or by happenstance. It only comes into being through a conscious choice made by inspired and determined hospital leadership—*like yourself!*

So mission statements must not be ignored or treated with disrespect. Unfortunately, my experience and research also proves that many hospitals don't devote enough serious attention to this vital component during their strategic planning process. They are continuing to commit too many **mission mistakes**. Indeed, my on-going work on hospital mission statements continues to show that most are surprisingly deficient in terms of the kinds of information they must contain. As a result, many hospitals are short-changing their own efforts to secure the **performance benefits** that can only accrue from being *mission-driven*.

I should stress here that creating a well-constructed mission statement is just the first of many essential steps that must be taken if your hospital is to become mission-driven. Other steps include determining:

- the impetus for creating your mission in the first place;
- how your mission statement is disseminated effectively so that it is understood, accepted and remembered by all employees and other key stakeholders; and

- how your hospital aligns all organizational systems and processes to reflect and reinforce the priorities contained in your mission statement.

This book, therefore, was written not just to point out the *conundrum* associated with mission statements but to give your hospital the tools it needs to become truly *mission-driven*. As the foundation for doing so, you'll find in Chapters 1 and 2 an introduction to—and overview of—**the unique and proprietary framework** that I developed from 12 years of studying the qualities, characteristics and processes that define mission-driven hospitals

The remaining chapters then discuss in more detail **the specific steps** your hospital must follow to establish its mission and carry it out. These sections are full of insights that I discovered while doing the major research project that informs this book. The steps are described within the context of what I call *The 5-C Mission Model*, which shows that for your hospital to become mission-driven, its leadership must give equal attention to:

- the process by which your mission is Created;
- the specific Content of your mission;
- the way in which your mission is Communicated (and to whom);
- how your mission is Coordinated ; and
- how your mission is Controlled.

The goal of each chapter is for you to use my findings *to immediately begin improving your hospital's performance.*

There are also **five mini (disguised) case histories** to illustrate the successes that hospitals have experienced in their efforts to become mission-driven. My hope is that they will encourage you and your hospital to make the mission statement not only popular but a highly effective management tool that produces *sustained successful performance.*

ONE

Making Mission Matter
The Mission-Driven Imperative

AS DISCUSSED IN THE FOREWORD, a *mission-driven hospital* is an organization in which everyone—*from the Boardroom to the bedside*—knows about, understands completely and commits passionately to achieving the aspirations, intentions, goals and objectives contained in the mission. It's an organization in which everyone can see clearly, exactly, precisely and unambiguously what it is that they have to do, both personally AND collectively, to help transform the mission statement from just a bunch of nice sounding words into a palpable *experience reality*, one that everyone can actually *feel*.

Why is it important for hospital administrators and their boards of directors to want this type of organization? Because when a hospital is not mission-driven, it becomes an organization without a clearly shared focus. It becomes a group of individuals—not a team—that lacks a collective sense of the whole. As a result, each person in the hospital develops their own individual 'game plan' which may have nothing to do with the hospital's mission or what anyone else is doing and, at worst, actually works against the mission and efforts of others. The mission-driven hospital therefore brings order to chaos and a sense of mission that drives and inspires individual performance for the benefit of all key *stakeholders*.

So how do you turn your hospital into a *mission-driven* organization?

To do this, we need to start with an *unambiguous* definition of what a mission statement is actually supposed to be and then move into a discussion of the four key components that *must* be in the mission statement of any hospital wanting to reap the rewards that come from being mission-driven.

PART 1

What Is This Thing Called "Mission"?

Definitions of the term **mission** abound! Here are just a few:

- In religion, a mission can mean a number of things, such as: (a) an evangelical or spirited gathering designed to bring participants back into the fold; (b) a religious structure (physical) or religious presence in a geographical area designed to teach, convert, and inspire individuals to follow a given religious persuasion; or (c) the journey or actions that a missionary carries out to persuade and inspire individuals to follow his/her faith.
- Mission also has military connotations. For example, soldiers carry out a mission, or action, designed to achieve a military goal.
- The *Oxford English Dictionary* offers four basic meanings for "mission": (a) "a particular task or goal assigned to a person or group; (b) a military or scientific operation or expedition for a particular purpose; (c) a body of persons sent, esp. to a foreign country, to conduct negotiations, etc; or (d) a body sent to propagate a religious faith".

While there are many other definitions of mission statements around representing various historical roots, one that I coined many years ago—and which is today becoming generally accepted—is that:

"a mission statement is *a formal written document intended to capture an organization's unique and enduring purpose and core values.*"

As such, a good mission statement answers one of the most fundamental questions that **every** organization—and therefore every hospital—needs to ask itself:

What is our essential reason for being? Or, put more simply, why do we exist?

So…why does <u>any</u> organization exist?

PART 2

The Four Key Components of a Mission Statement for a Mission-Driven Hospital

Obviously, no organization can exist if it does not meet the basic requirement of survival, which is "to make money." Or in the case of all not-for-profit hospitals: "to break even." Breaking even, of course, can mean either making enough revenue to cover expenses or managing expenses to live within the revenues available.

The reason for-profit institutions need to be increasingly profitable is relatively straightforward: such firms must demonstrate to their shareholders/investors the ability to *meet their needs*—usually by providing a sufficient (and increasing) ROI (return on investment). When this occurs, the firm is able to **attract and retain investors** **(ARI)** whose continued financing (i.e. loyalty) is absolutely essential in order to fund future growth. Why is this so important? Because if a firm does not grow, its competitors will get larger and stronger by default. And, over time, it will not exist.

While there is no such pressure on hospitals to produce profits, there still is, however, an expectation they will use their resources responsibly, particularly when the hospital's operations are partially (or substantially) funded by governments, foundations and philanthropic donors.

Thus, one of the primary reasons hospitals exist is because they *are able to attract and retain funders by meeting and satisfying their needs for fiscal prudence or conscientious stewardship.* And the mission statement is one vital way of communicating to financial backers (as well as to those responsible for making it happen) that the hospital is aware of this need and dedicated to its fulfillment.

Consider the missions of three representative healthcare institutions (**Pennsylvania Hospital** in Philadelphia, Pennsylvania; **The Mayo Clinic** in Rochester, Minnesota; and the **Sacred Heart Hospital** in Allentown, Pennsylvania—**see Box Inset** at the end of this Chapter), each of which meets the first test of a good mission statement for a mission-driven hospital:

- Pennsylvania Hospital's mission, for instance, is to "exhibit stewardship and creativity in the management of all available resources";
- The Mayo Clinic says it will "operate in a manner intended not to create wealth but to provide a financial return sufficient for present and future needs";
- Sacred Heart, a religious, faith-based institution, proclaims it will "assure that the system will remain viable by providing cost effective and value-driven services... [and] a program of continuous performance improvement."

However, breaking even is not the only element in defining *the purpose* of not-for-profit organizations, such as hospitals. A good mission statement also reveals (again to its funders) **how** the organization intends to fulfill its financial obligations and, in so doing, provides greater amplification to the question of *why it exists*. The late management guru Peter Drucker once said the purpose of any organization is "to create a customer." In that wonderful phrase, he managed to capture an essential ingredient of any organization's long-term success: *no customer, no revenues, no business.*

But how does any organization go about *attracting and retaining a customer (ARC)* to get the revenues it requires to at least cover its expenses (and ideally provide a financial return)? The answer to this question is fairly simple and should be well known to most hospitals: *The key to obtaining and keeping your patient-clients lies in identifying, meeting and exceeding their needs and expectations greater than existing providers—and by doing so on a continuous, reliable basis.*

A good mission statement, therefore, **vividly portrays** in considerable detail (using carefully chosen words) just how your hospital intends to do the above. Armed with this information, potential funders can readily assess if what your hospital is proposing as its "business model" makes sense and if it truly captures what your patient-clients are currently lacking. However, if hospital leadership consistently misses the mark in terms of identifying those *competitively distinguishing* aspects then your institution will, over time, eventually cease to exist—or at least in its current form.

Such is not the case with the three hospital examples featured in this chapter. Each mission statement offers the kind of thoughtful and colorful picture about patient care to which every healthcare organization should aspire. In other words, each successfully gives both patient-clients and funders a sense of confidence in the hospital's understanding of what unfulfilled needs must be met—and, ideally, surpassed. All three clearly and succinctly succeed in this second test of a good mission statement for a mission-driven hospital:

- Pennsylvania Hospital's mission states that it "has a responsibility to ensure access to superior quality integrated healthcare";
- The Mayo Clinic proclaims it will "provide the best care to every patient every day through integrated clinical practice, education and research. The needs of the patient come first."
- Sacred Heart's mission provides assurance that it "is committed to provide healthcare and wellness, from conception to natural death, through quality services and programs based on the Catholic ethical and religious directives...(the hospital) recognizes the dignity and eternal destiny of each individual with special concern for the sick and the poor."

There is, of course, a world of difference between saying what you want to do for a patient-client and actually doing it. But, let's now go back to the *conundrum* discussed in the Foreword to this book.

Delivering consistently on a demanding brand promise (such as the high aspirations for patient satisfaction, happiness and even fulfillment that can be found in our three mission statement examples) requires *considerable effort, energy, passion, dedication and commitment—particularly from your front line employees—in order to make it happen.* And yet consider some of the ugly facts about employee commitment and engagement that have been reported at various times:

- 47% of 30,000 employees surveyed said they dislike going to work
- According to Gallup, 80% of U.S. workers dread going to work
- Fewer than 1 out of every 4 job holders say they are currently working at full potential
- One half said they do not put more effort into their job than what is required to hang onto it
- A Conference Board's study indicated that 43% of companies surveyed reported difficulties in *finding and retaining* high-quality people.

And no wonder. The workplace can be a particularly brutal and soul-sapping environment:

So how does a hospital go about obtaining the kind of energy and commitment it requires from its workforce in order to deliver on its promises to its patient-clients?

In what may be a surprise to many of you, my research and consulting indicates the answer to that question starts by recognizing that **patient-client needs are best satisfied when employee needs are well satisfied, too.**

A good mission statement for the mission-driven hospital, therefore, describes what your employees can expect to receive from your organization *in exchange for* their **willingness** to **commit and submit** to delivering the institution's brand promise—with excellence. Consequently, your hospital's mission statement must show what your organization will do to **attract and retain employees (ARE)**, thus changing a *hostile* environment, as suggested by the ugly facts above, into a *hospitable* one.

Consider now these passages from the missions of our three example hospitals, each of which passes the third test of a good mission statement for the mission-driven hospital:

- Pennsylvania Hospital's mission talks about creating "a supportive team environment for…employees and clinical staff";
- The Mayo Clinic says it will "treat everyone in our diverse community with respect and dignity" while encouraging "teamwork, personal responsibility, integrity, innovation, trust and communication";
- And Sacred Heart's mission promises to provide a work environment characterized by "meaningful employment, education and training to our employees"

But wait, as they say on TV infomercials, there's more…

There's a **new ingredient** to a good mission statement that has emerged through my research to help explain why any organization —including a hospital—exists (and what it needs to do to continue to exist). This new component **concerns *an organization's degree of commitment to being ethically and socially responsible***—and it is gaining more and more influence.

But why is this now so important? There are two reasons for this. The first is that *"society" itself is emerging as a separate and distinct stakeholder.* It is becoming clear that all organizations today generally need some sort of 'permit' or 'social license' from the communities in which they operate in order to conduct their business. But obtaining—and holding onto—that "piece of paper" is no longer automatic. Accordingly, wise organizations are now also demonstrating a willingness to **attract and retain the goodwill of others** in society *(ARGO)—and thereby obtain the necessary permits—by being exemplary corporate citizens.*

The second reason? Organizations are becoming more and more concerned about what others think about them. In other words: *their public reputation* is becoming increasingly important to them. This is because there is now a recognition that real performance advantages can be gained by those organizations with strong reputations for delivering on the promises contained in their mission statements and other brand messages. In other words, organizations with highly positive reputations outperform those with lesser ones. Some of the significant performance differences noted between "high" versus "low" reputation firms include the following:

Reputation is Tied to Financial Performance		
Performance Criteria	Reputation Rating	
	Low	High
Cost of goods sold	60.8	49.0
Employment growth	2.8%	6.9%
Net Margin	4.3	8.0
Return on assets	4.3%	8.4%
Cash flow to sales	12.8	18.1
Price-earnings ratio	21.7	32.5
Return on equity	16.8	38.4
EPS growth	7.3	24.8
Revenues per employee	$2.46M	$4.55M

SOURCE: Fombrun & Van Riel, 2004, p.78

Additionally, when your organization is socially responsible and develops a good public reputation, it becomes a *source of pride* for employees, patient-clients and funders alike. Individually and collectively, these stakeholders do not want to associate themselves with organizations that are not good corporate citizens. Thus, any hospital that ignores or actively abuses the trust that society as a whole has placed in it will see more and more stakeholders withdraw their support.

It is for these reasons that the mission statements of our three sample hospitals express their concern for good citizenship and/or ethical conduct—and by so doing meet the fourth and final 'content test' of a good mission statement for a mission-driven hospital:

- **Pennsylvania Hospital's** mission declares that it is responsible for "expand(ing) access for underserved populations within the community...(and) "foster[ing] learning and growth through comprehensive academic and educational relationships";
- **The Mayo Clinic** mission says it will "benefit humanity through patient care, education and research. Support the

communities in which we live and work. Serve appropriately patients in difficult financial circumstances";
- **Sacred Heart's** mission proclaims that "Our healthcare network continues its leadership in the community through collaboration and affiliation with recognized regional and national experts."

What all the above suggests is that the best answer to the question of "Why does any organization exist" is this: *because it is able to satisfy and exceed the needs of its multiple stakeholders.*

Accordingly, the content of a great mission statement for a mission-driven hospital articulates the critical success factors that make the organization viable and, in so doing, expresses what the hospital intends to do for its various stakeholders *in exchange for* their continuing loyalty and support. Or, put slightly differently, the definition of a great mission statement, such as the ones depicted here, is that it:

> *Describes the relationships that a hospital needs to create, maintain and enhance with those stakeholders (i.e., client-patients, funders/investors, employees and society at large) who are critical to the organization's continued success and survival.*

Given this definition, taking a cookie-cutter approach to hospital mission statements by "borrowing and adapting" someone else's simply will not do. (More on this later!).

To get a better understanding of a hospital's various relationships, see Figure 1 which shows that not only are individual stakeholders in their own unique relationship with the hospital but *they are also inextricably in relationships with one another.*

Yes, your hospital must still meet and satisfy each stakeholder's needs if it's to continue enjoying their individual loyalty and support. However, the **ah-ha insight** that Figure 1 also reveals is that there is a "satisfaction relationship chain"—linking funders, patient-clients, employees and society.

What this means in practical terms is that it would be extremely difficult to satisfy funders without having satisfied:

- Patients-clients (who are the source of the hospital's revenues and reputation);
- Employees (who are the source of the hospital's excellence in patient care); and
- Society (which brings 'pride of association' to the hospital)

It would also be extremely difficult to satisfy patient-clients over the long term without having both satisfied employees and a positive reputation with the greater community. After all, who wants to have services supplied by a hospital with questionable ethics? And it would be especially difficult to have satisfied employees if they are ashamed to work for the hospital because of its bad reputation.

Thus, as my research has discovered: *not all missions are created equal*. And the failure to consider and address any of the four major stakeholder needs in your hospital's mission statement should constitute an *early-warning signal* about your organization's long-term ability to exist.

Armed with a properly constituted mission statement, such as the ones discussed here, a hospital—your hospital!—is now well-positioned to take the additional steps necessary to becoming truly *mission-driven*.

PART 3

"Mission" Versus "Vision"

At the start of this chapter, I provided an unambiguous definition of "mission." At this point, it would be useful to do similarly for "vision" because, after all, a mission statement can't be the same as a vision statement. And so, my definition of organizational vision is that it is:

a massively inspiring, overarching long-term goal.

Figure 1

Hospitals Have a Variety of Stakeholders Whose Needs They Must Address

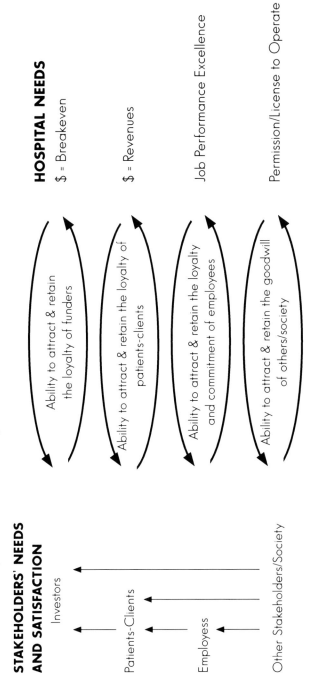

Here are three good examples of hospital vision statements:

- Patton State Hospital in Sacramento, California has a desire "to lead in the recovery of individuals in need of psychiatric care";
- John F. Kennedy Memorial Hospital in Indio, California has as its goal "to become the first choice for health and medical services for residents of the Eastern Coachella Valley"; and
- St Michael's Hospital in Toronto, Ontario, believes that "through its culture of caring and discovery, St Michael's will be Canada's finest academic healthcare provider".

Vision statements are generally comprised of only one sentence and are typically concerned with achieving *greatness* or *leadership* in some dimension, such as reputation, patient care, research, etc. Because of its lofty aim, the vision goal invariably takes a long time to accomplish—often ten years or more.

A mission statement, on the other hand, expresses *what your hospital intends to do day-in-and-day-out* and—if successful—*helps make its vision attainable*. As such, a mission statement represents the **platform** by which a hospital will reach towards its vision. Indeed, it would be virtually impossible for any hospital to achieve its vision without a well-executed mission.

PART 4

A "Mission-driven" Overview

The concept of being *mission-driven* as described in this book is represented diagrammatically in Figure 2 the next page.

As Figure 2 shows, the mission statement of a mission-driven hospital is responsible for driving and influencing all actions and tasks within all departments and functions. Being "**mission-driven**", therefore, means that your hospital's mission statement becomes *the cornerstone and primary influencer of all decisions and behaviors that take place throughout the organization and at all levels. That's because it has been **integrated completely** throughout your hospital.*

Figure 2: Being Mission-Driven

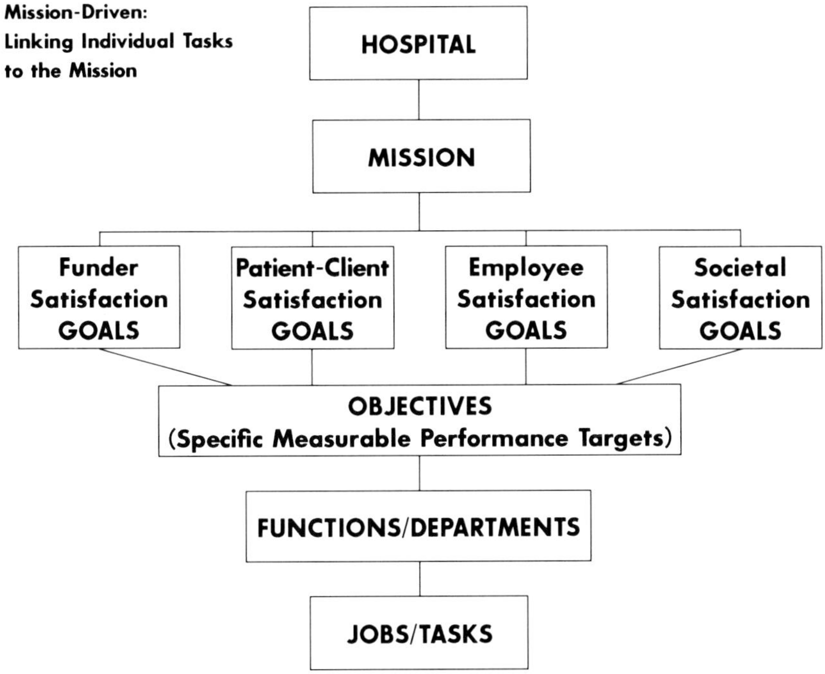

Mission-Driven:
Linking Individual Tasks
to the Mission

```
                        HOSPITAL
                           |
                        MISSION
                           |
  +-----------+-----------+-----------+-----------+
  Funder     Patient-Client  Employee    Societal
Satisfaction  Satisfaction  Satisfaction Satisfaction
  GOALS        GOALS          GOALS        GOALS

            OBJECTIVES
 (Specific Measurable Performance Targets)

        FUNCTIONS/DEPARTMENTS

              JOBS/TASKS
```

An important aspect of making this happen occurs first through the *translation* of your hospital's mission into a series of goals and objectives. These "mission-driven performance metrics" ultimately cascade their way down throughout your hospital whereby every person—especially the front line—has a sense of *understanding* __and__ *ownership* as to what the mission statement means for them in their particular job. Moreover, every person will see the direct connection between what they are doing (and what everyone else is doing) *on a daily basis* and how it makes a difference in terms of your hospital achieving its mission—or not!

The 5-C Mission Model—which was introduced in the Foreword and is explained in more detail in the next chapter—provides a bullet-proof, step-by-step guide that shows exactly what your hospital must do to become mission-driven.

Let's now delve more deeply into the details of this powerful performance enhancing framework.

THREE EXCELLENT EXAMPLES
OF HOSPITAL MISSION STATEMENTS

Sacred Heart HealthCare System Mission Statement

Sacred Heart HealthCare System is committed to provide health-care and wellness, from conception to natural death, through quality services and programs based on the Catholic ethical and religious directives.

Our healthcare network continues its leadership in the community through collaboration and affiliation with recognized regional and national experts.

We assure that the system will remain viable by providing cost effective and value-driven services. A program of continuous performance improvement enables us to respond to the needs of the community while giving meaningful employment, education and training to our employees.

In fulfilling this mission, Sacred Heart HealthCare System recognizes the dignity and eternal destiny of each individual with special concern for the sick and the poor.

Source: http://www.shh.org/about-us/mission-statement.asp

The Mayo Clinic's Mission

Mayo Clinic will provide the best care to every patient every day through integrated clinical practice, education and research.

Primary Value

The needs of the patient come first.

Core Principles

Practice	Practice medicine as an integrated team of compassionate, multi-disciplinary physicians, scientists and allied health professionals who are focused on the needs of patients from our communities, regions, the nation and the world.
Education	Educate physicians, scientists and allied health professionals and be a dependable source of health information for our patients and the public.
Research	Conduct basic and clinical research programs to improve patient care and to benefit society.
Mutual Respect	Treat everyone in our diverse community with respect and dignity.
Commitment to Quality	Continuously improve all processes that support patient care, education and research.
Work Atmosphere	Foster teamwork, personal responsibility, integrity, innovation, trust and communication within the context of a physician-led institution.
Societal Commitment	Benefit humanity through patient care, education and research. Support the communities in which we live and work. Serve appropriately patients in difficult financial circumstances.
Finances	Allocate resources within the context of a system rather than its individual entities. Operate in a manner intended not to create wealth but to provide a financial return sufficient for present and future needs.

SOURCE: http://www.mayoclinic.org/careerawareness/mi-mission.html

The Mission Statement of Pennsylvania Hospital

We believe that Pennsylvania Hospital, the nation's first hospital, has a responsibility to:

- Ensure access to superior quality integrated healthcare for our community and expand access for underserved populations within the community
- Create a supportive team environment for patients, employees, and clinical staff
- Foster learning and growth through comprehensive academic and educational relationships
- Exhibit stewardship and creativity in the management of all available resources

SOURCE: http://www.pennmedicine.org/pahosp/about/mission.html

TWO

A Model Mission

The Critical Success Factors Behind
the "5-C" Mission Model or *If you can only
read one chapter, read this one!!*

EVIDENCE FROM MY NUMEROUS STUDIES suggests the major
reason for *mission failure* is the way in which mission initiatives are
undertaken and carried out. In fact, my research into hospitals and
other organizations shows there are *critical factors in mission development and implementation* that need to be carefully planned and executed in order to create a genuine mission-driven organization. This,
therefore, requires a *winning mission process*, one which is meaningful—not just in theory—but is operable and ultimately makes a difference in the practices of the organization.

    *What is that winning method or process that can transform an ordi-
nary hospital into a mission-driven one?* The answer is not found in
magic or sleight of hand but rather in an integrated and comprehensive set of activities: my **5-C Mission Model**, with its emphasis on
Creation, Content, Communication, Coordination and Control.

Creation: Getting Mission Off To A 'Big Bang'

The Creation of a mission statement should begin by figuring out why your hospital wants to embark upon a mission exercise in the first place. After all, your hospital might decide to undertake the development of a mission for a number of reasons:

- To provide a sense of *purpose and direction* to your hospital and its members so that it can avoid distractions in a turbulent operating environment;
- To ensure that the *interests of key stakeholders* are being met (key stakeholders include funders, patients-clients, employees and the community);
- To *sharpen your hospital's focus* so its members can concentrate on key business and core competencies and thereby become the best it can be in those areas;
- To *enable better control over employees*, ensuring that hospital members act in line with stated goals and objectives; and/or
- To *promote shared values and behavioral standards* among stakeholders by defining and declaring your hospital's operational philosophy.

All of these *rationales* (and others that could be cited) are valid reasons for your hospital to try to create its mission statement. As you will notice, each of these rationales is different yet similar: they all deal with the **focus and direction of the hospital** and they are all concerned with **enlisting stakeholders** in developing a shared purpose in mission.

This first "C"—Creation—therefore focuses on understanding why developing a mission statement is necessary in the first place. It is not sufficient simply to remember that mission statements are the precursor to strategy formulation. Rather, they must be seen as the essential power (*the elan vital*) behind successful strategic planning. Accordingly, a mission defines a hospital's most important organizational goals; **it is the first and essential component of any quality strategic plan.**

Recognizing what your hospital's rationale is for developing a mission will lead you to appropriate decisions about the Content of your mission statement and how it should ultimately be Communicated, Coordinated and Controlled. However, Creation is not just about defining rationale—or the *Why we are going to spend all this time deciding on what we want the mission to do for us?*—but it is also about the *How*, and delineating the process by which your mission exercise will be undertaken.

Creation, therefore, also involves *action*. My research has shown that the way in which the **mission Creation *process*** is inaugurated and carried out in hospitals is an essential determinant of its ultimate success. As a leader of a hospital, your ultimate 'leadership goal' is to inspire and motivate your hospital's employees and others to exceptional performance. Fortunately, this is one of the powerful potential outcomes of a successful mission exercise. Accordingly, a great Creation process, therefore, means actively *engaging* your hospital's staff and other key stakeholders in the mission's development and having them embrace it.

Intuitively the idea that participation *should* affect behavior (even if via an intermediary variable) seems a sound one. So it's no wonder that the management literature is rife with discussions on participation, participatory management, employee empowerment and other management tools to engage and motivate employees. The common theme is that **participation helps to engender buy-in and commitment** which, by the way, is why the budgeting activity has been decentralized and pushed to lower levels of the organization. The theory goes as follows: if I devise a budget, I will commit to it, especially if my performance is being evaluated on how well I fulfill my proposed budget. In essence, enlisting participation is a commitment device. By your participation and that of others, we get to know what everyone thinks and believes. We can then be guided to an overall consensus which, in turn, helps to enhance 'goal congruity' throughout the organization.

For mission acceptance, participation is especially crucial. This means that the Creation phase must involve give and take throughout the mission process, not just a photo-opportunity announcement of the *fait accompli*—the finished mission statement. Most would agree that **there are many stakeholder groups who have a legitimate interest in the mission process**—the board of directors (or governors), the CEO, senior management, middle management, front-line employees (non-managers), shareholders/funders, patients-clients, and suppliers, to name a few. All of these require continuing engagement throughout the mission Creation process.

To date, my research is the only one that has linked various hospital performance outcomes (e.g. 'satisfaction with the mission development process', 'commitment to the mission', 'the impact of mission as an energy source' and 'guide for decision making') with varying degrees of stakeholders' participation. My findings show that (not unexpectedly) it is the CEO, board and senior managers who are typically—and almost exclusively—involved in the mission process while other stakeholders are largely ignored. Surprisingly, my research also uncovered the fact that the involvement of the CEO in the mission process had less of an impact on various hospital performance outcome measures than the involvement of middle managers, funders/shareholders and patients-customers.

Seeking wide stakeholder participation, then, appears to be an important part of the mission process; the mission statement will benefit from having a broad assortment of perspectives and the stakeholders will feel a greater sense of ownership in the finished mission statement.

However, notwithstanding the importance of stakeholder participation, the *style of your mission Creation process* has a significant influence on the degree to which the mission is enthusiastically accepted. My research has found that a good Creation process style is one that will transcend the autocratic dictation of mission to the underlings (the classic top-down approach). To enhance buy-in, the style needs to be both *flexible* and somewhat *informal* and employ a relatively *simple* process that proceeds creatively. Indeed, sticking rigidly to an assigned time-table will be deleterious to the outcome! Only when the mission statement is believed to have widespread acceptance and support (through a show of hands or ballot) should the Creation process *related to the finalization of the mission's content* be considered completed.

Thus, hospitals need to think hard and deeply about *process* so that their mission Creation endeavour goes beyond self-indulgent navel-gazing and becomes a dynamic means of engaging hospital stakeholders.

As discussed earlier, the major defects of mission statements are that they are either not taken seriously or they are ignored. Both of these problems can be traced back to inadequacies in the Creation process when, for example, the hospital was not sufficiently aware of why it was developing its mission, or it used a poor or non-existent process to bring the mission statement into existence. Both errors can derail a hospital's attempt to become *mission-driven*.

Thus, process does matter! And, not coincidentally, the entire 5-C model itself involves having the right process for mission development, dissemination and alignment. This is why the **5-C Mission Model must be seen as an integrated whole**—each C of the model is related to and needs the other Cs. While it makes sense to describe Creation as the starting point, the other Cs of the Mission Model (Content, Communication, Coordination and Control) all emanate from the rationales and creation process agreed on in the initiating stage.

Content: Finding The Right Words

Of all the research investigations into mission statements, **the topic most frequently studied has been their content and composition.** Most of this research to date, however, has been nothing more than simple frequency counts of the different categories of information that can occur. The fault with such an approach is this: There are numerous potential categories—my research has revealed up to 40 different mission content "items" in studies by different authors— none of which is well-correlated with actual performance. In other words, there is little historical advice as to which items *should be/ must be* included in a mission. However, since the purpose of the mission imperative is to affect hospital performance and to affect it positively, having the right mission content should be important. So, **mission content cannot be taken lightly**.

My research into 'corporate' mission statements abandoned the frequency counts of mission statement items for a better approach: tracking the correlation between 22 mission content items (Exhibit 1) and company performance *measured by* such tangible indicators as 'return on sales' (i.e., net income divided by sales dollars times 100%) and 'growth in profits' (i.e., profit in year 2 divided by profit in year 1, minus 1, times 100%).

My research shows that *not all mission content is equally important*. Indeed, **some mission-statement items appear to be clearly and equivocally associated with high performance**, thereby making a difference to the final product, while others are not. Furthermore, the appropriate content of mission statements is *related to an organization's industry*. For example, and not surprisingly, the meaningful content of a successful hospital mission statement differs from that of a high-technology firm or an airline company. More specifically, high-tech firms prefer to leave their definition of business very loose so as not to confine or restrict the application of their technology. As well, the mission statement of a high-tech firm is distinguished by the degree to which it specifies certain important behavioral standards, such as 'satisfying difficult customers', 'promoting an egalitarian workplace', 'recruiting the right people' and 'glorifying innovators'.

In the case of not-for-profit hospitals, **eight mission components were among the most powerful** in terms of their relation to measures of *mission-driven-ness*: distinctive competence; specification of patients-clients served; specification of services/products offered; unique identity; concern for satisfying patients-clients, concern for satisfying employees; concern for society; and, concern for shareholders/owners/funders.

As can readily be seen, most of these items inherently possess potential emotive power—the ability to evoke passionate responses from stakeholder groups. Hence, **mission statements that matter capture content that moves both the hearts and minds of managers, front-line employees, patients-clients and funders alike.** As well, successful mission statements are simple and relatively short (especially in the early years) so that their message is potent and understandable. However, it should be pointed out that as an organization grows and matures, so too may its mission statement. Take for example the current mission of Johnson and Johnson (Exhibit 2). After 65 years of use and ongoing refinement, it has emerged into a substantial and long statement that still, remarkably, every one of their employees can actually recite.

Warning! Developing a mission statement certainly takes time and, to be effective, a broad representation of organizational participants should be involved. All of this, of course, costs money, thereby making mission statements expensive both in their direct costs and their opportunity cost. Because of this, hospitals face the dilemma of whether to start afresh and create their own mission statements or to study others' to see what they can adopt or adapt from them.

Efficiency and expense would, at first glance, suggest that "borrowing" is good. By using another hospital's mission statement as the template for your own, you need not recreate the wheel; you'd simply be working from a "live" mission document currently in force. It's a common thought.

However, simply imitating another hospital's mission statement or engaging in a top-down prescription of the mission simply will not work. Too often in the past, for example, researchers have found that the supposedly "model" or "winning" mission statements included in their books and articles are the products of "losing" companies by the time their work is in print. Enron and WorldCom had what seemed to be viable mission statements but no organization today would conceive of adapting them out of hand.

Another problem with such "borrowing," whether from other hospitals' mission statements or from research findings, is that comparable content is just not sufficient to establish the mission for any one particular organization. **Each hospital needs to discover, to choose—and buy into—the appropriate content for itself (i.e., the specific and deliberately chosen words which uniquely describes and defines that hospital's overall purpose as well as the ends and means it will pursue to achieve that purpose).**

Admittedly, the content of mission statements is, in the extreme, *generic* but at the same time it has to be *specific to the hospital*. Indeed, my research over the years has shown that, in addition to firm or industry considerations, subtle differences in content can have profound differences in the effectiveness of mission statements. As a

EXHIBIT 1

**Potential Mission Statement Content Components
(Non-ranked)**

1. Statement of purpose (what are we ultimately trying to accomplish that makes what we do worthwhile? What is our grand aim?)
2. Statement of values/beliefs/philosophy (What kind of personal values would we like to define our organization and work environment?)
3. Distinctive competence (What are the distinctive strengths of the organization (current or intended) upon which we should build our strategy?)
4. Desired competitive position (What is our position relative to the competition and how should we seek to improve it?)
5. Competitive strategy (How do we (intend to) attract and retain customers?)
6. Behavioral standards
7. General corporate goals
8. One clear and compelling goal
9. Specific financial performance targets/objectives
10. Specific non-financial performance targets/objectives
11. Specific patients-clients served
12. Specific services/products offered
13. Unique identity/self concept (Are our products and/or customers different from other competitors?)
14. Desired public image (How do we want others to see us?)
15. Identification of the business location
16. Definition of technology used (to be used)
17. Concern for future/long term survival
18. Concern for patients-clients
19. Concern for employees and their welfare
20. Concern for suppliers
21. Concern for society
22. Concern for shareholders/owners/funders

EXHIBIT 2

Our Credo

We believe our first responsibility is to the doctors, nurses, and patients,
to mothers and fathers and all others who use our products and services.
In meeting their needs everything we do must be of high quality.
We must constantly strive to reduce our costs
in order to maintain reasonable prices.
Customers' orders must be serviced promptly and accurately.
Our suppliers and distributors must have an opportunity
to make a fair profit.

We are responsible to our employees, the men and women who work with us through-
out the world.
Everyone must be considered as an individual.
We must respect their dignity and recognize their merit.
They must have a sense of security in their jobs.
Compensation must be fair and adequate, and working conditions clean,
orderly and safe.
We must be mindful of ways to help our employees fulfill
their family responsibilities.
Employees must feel free to make suggestions and complaints.
There must be equal opportunity for employment, development
and advancement for those qualified.

We must provide competent management, and their actions must be just and ethical.
We are responsible to the communities in which we live and work
and to the world community as well.
We must be good citizens —support good works and charities
and bear our fair share of taxes.
We must encourage civic improvements and better health and education.
We must maintain in good order the property we are privileged to use,
protecting the environment and natural resources.

Our final responsibility is to our stockholders.
Business must make a sound profit.
We must experiment with new ideas.
Research must be carried on, innovative programs developed and mistakes paid for.
New equipment must be purchased, new facilities provided
and new products launched.
Reserves must be created to provide for adverse times.
When we operate according to these principles,
the stockholders should realize a fair return.

Johnson&Johnson

result, effective hospital mission statements have a *unique signature* which a simple "borrowing" cannot reproduce.

Communication: Enlisting the Troops

Even if you are convinced your hospital has a valid rationale for its mission exercise and you have drafted a mission statement that captures salient components, such as behavioral expectations and stakeholders' needs, your efforts will be doomed to failure unless you continuously *engage* the organization in the mission. *Education* in and *continual* Communication of the mission throughout the entire hospital is therefore an essential step for making the mission 'real' for the troops—especially the front line. In fact, in one of my research studies, Communication proved to be more important than Content in motivating performance.

Interestingly, when people think of Communication, they usually list the standard things: e-mails, memos, plaques, posters, town-hall meetings, videos and newsletters, among others. But, Communication has a more fundamental meaning here, connoting not only *the medium* but also *the effect* it has. In other words, it's one thing to Communicate. It's a completely different matter to Communicate effectively.

To be communicated effectively, mission statements must be concise, straightforward and clear. Without clarity and straightforwardness, the import of your mission statement's messages is obfuscated. Indeed, how can you hope to inspire someone if he or she does not understand what they are reading or hearing? Moreover, if the message is not clear and concise, people will not remember the mission. And if they don't remember the mission, it's as if it's never been sent! Accordingly, it is important to ask: what **methods** of Communicating the mission—and the messages contained in it—are effective? Are some Communication methods more effective than others so that the mission has a real impact on the organization and its members.

My own research on mission Communication within hospitals has recently discovered that multiple meetings which allow questions, websites that encourage feedback, campaigns that involve "rolling out" the mission, and especially **word-of-mouth 'supervisor initi-ated' discussions of the mission** (that show how *both individual jobs and departmental initiatives are related to and reinforce the mission*) are all ways of improving understanding and truly Communicating a mission's message Content.

Communication is thus a critical factor in gaining commitment to the mission. However, Communication cannot end once the mission statement's final Content has been accepted. To inspire stakeholders and ensure that the mission is in fact carried out, the mission process items of Coordination and Control must come into play, two aspects of the **5-C Model** that keep Communication of your hospital's mission front and centre throughout the entire organization.

Coordination: Aligning a Hospital's 'Organization' With Its Mission

Mission initiatives with their resultant mission statements often incur rancour and dissatisfaction from many of a hospital's constituents even though the entity's "missionaries" appeared to do everything right in defining both the reasons for the mission's Creation and the Content of the mission. They may also have Communicated with their stakeholders properly and launched their mission to general applause. What happens then? The mission becomes a document like any other in the hospital, sterile and inoperative, *unless* specific additional steps are taken to help it become part of every-day organizational life.

Unfortunately too many hospital missionaries believe their brand new mission statement—by itself—is sufficient to motivate employees (especially at the 'front line') and to inspire its achievement. They incorrectly assume that organizational life—the formal and informal systems which underlie operations—will automatically subsume (i.e. reflect and reinforce) the mission. They don't. In fact, hospital constituents will become frustrated and disillusioned with their organization's mission if the systems and structures they work under do not *overtly* promulgate the mission and the goals embedded in it.

What's needed then is a mission that genuinely becomes part of the daily, on-going operations and activities of the hospital—*one that is completely integrated throughout the hospital*. To make this happen, the mission statement needs to be referred to and consulted in meetings between employees and managers; the mission must become *embedded* into every staff member's job and job description; plans, budgets and business objectives need to *invoke and reflect the mission statement*; and training systems need to be developed using the mission statement as guide for the skills and behaviors required. These particular organizational activities and systems serve to give life to the mission with which they are <u>C</u>oordinated—or *aligned*. <u>C</u>oordination also further advances the <u>C</u>ommunication of the mission by making it continuously visible through its organizational structures.

When the mission statement is just a nice shiny plaque that hangs on your hospital's lobby wall, it is virtually worthless. But when it is aligned with your hospital's systems and resources, the result is a champion organization that outstrips competitors who have not developed the same degree of focus, dedication and commitment.

<u>C</u>oordination, the fourth <u>C</u> of the Mission Model, is thus critical to sustaining the life of the mission statement. Without the proper "fit" or alignment of mission with management systems, the benefits of the mission initiative suffer an early demise. With <u>C</u>oordination, however, the driving force of mission is put in high gear **and the mission-driven hospital begins to emerge.**

Control: Insurance that the Mission Stays the Course

<u>C</u>ontrol, the fifth and final <u>C</u> of the 5-C **Mission Model**, at once seems obvious yet is often overlooked. Throughout my description of the 5-C **Mission Model**, I have mentioned the need for flexibility, informality and creativity in the mission process. Sometimes these terms give a misleading message about the freedom and empowerment that employees need to have in a mission-driven organization.

Most philosophers or moralists will tell you there is a difference between freedom and licenses. Freedom implies that we may act without being unduly hampered or frustrated, whereas license implies liberty without any restraint (and which may sometimes involve breaking laws or abuse of special privilege). To be free to act therefore does not necessarily mean to do as one pleases, but rather to work within a framework of structures and systems *that guide behavior through information reporting, rewards and punishments.* In a sense, these structures and systems create the basis of society and define individuals' freedom.

Organizations, of course, develop many types of systems and in the mission-driven hospital some systems, as previously discussed, are there to reinforce the mission (i.e., they Coordinate it). My research has shown, however, that there are also other management systems which need to be *aligned* but *which are designed specifically to Control a hospital mission's implementation (thereby keeping the hospital focussed on the mission)*, namely: the 'information reporting' system (which shows hospital performance against mission-related strategic and operating plans and budgets); the 'reward/punishment' system (which should have mission-related performance evaluation criteria and rewards); the promotion system; the mission-related 'employee values' that hospitals seek to acquire through the recruitment system; and the mission-related behavioral examples offered through the 'leadership styles' of a hospital's senior executives. These systems and activities not only contain elements which *encourage* consideration of the mission goals in everyday decisions, but they also *reward (or punish) achievement (or non-achievement)* of those goals.

Mission performance outcomes thus matter to organizational members because there is both *tangible feedback* **and** *accountability* **for their actions.** It should be pointed out, though, that the 'outcome/ performance measurement/reward connection' does not mean only monetary awards but also other forms of recognition for achieving positive results. Studies of employee satisfaction, in particular, show that while adequate remuneration is necessary, it is not a sufficient reward. **Recognition of one's contribution** to the success of the mission through awards of many types serves to satisfy an employee's higher needs of self actualization. And such forms of Control also further reinforce and renew their commitment to the mission.

Control, therefore, is a fundamental requirement for the success of a hospital's mission and insures that its **internal stakeholders are all commonly connected, focussed and motivated.** When combined with its Coordination 'cousin', they together form the basis upon which **the mission-driven hospital—like steel—is forged and tempered.**

My research in particular has found that the strong alignment of the mission with a hospital's organizational systems and structures (which comes as a result of the Coordination and Control components of the **5-C Mission Model**) is one of the most powerful catalysts in transforming mission potency into action. It communicates forcefully to constituents the seriousness and significance the hospital believes the mission to hold. And it is an especially important way of engendering mission commitment and, consequently, enhancing performance. An interesting consequence is that those employees who cannot commit to their hospital's mission will probably ultimately choose to leave (due to lack of 'fit') while others who do believe in it will join. As stakeholders' commitment to a particular hospital mission grows, the long-term success of the mission—and satisfaction with it—grows likewise.

NOTE: Because of the high overlap in the components making up Coordination and Control—and because most components do "DOUBLE DUTY" in terms of furthering the aims of each concept—I have chosen to discuss them together going forward in future Chapters.

The "Bart Star"

The **5-C Mission Model** provides a basic road map to guide you in developing a mission-driven hospital. For hospitals and the healthcare sector in general, mission can be the difference between institutions with poor employee morale (whose only thought is day-to-day reaction to resource cut-backs) and those institutions with employees committed to common goals (whose resource decisions in a turbulent environment are guided by the goals set out in the mission).

Figure 3 summarizes what I call 'The Bart Star', a visual representation of the 5-C **Mission Model** and what needs to happen for your hospital to **integrate and implement its mission throughout your entire organization**. It's my unique framework—discovered after years of research—for turning your hospital's mission into reality. It especially illustrates—vividly and evocatively—the need to **align** all of your hospital's structures, systems, processes and activities to reflect, reinforce and facilitate the implementation of the mission.

As previously discussed, the process begins with the Creation and Content specification of your hospital's mission involving all key stakeholders. Thereafter, it is important to identify and Communicate (on an annual basis) *the critical priorities* contained in the mission that are most in need of your hospital's attention. While, ultimately, your hospital is responsible for carrying out all of the goals contained in its mission, no organization can focus on *doing everything with excellence at the same time*. Accordingly, your leadership challenge is to find those aspects of your hospital's mission in most need of attention and/or repair and, when these have been dealt with, turning your hospital's attention to other mission areas of concern.

Armed with three to five "mission-critical priorities," the next step is to Communicate and Coordinate responsibility for their implementation—or solution—to as many persons in the hospital as possible. This occurs by aligning your hospital's strategic and operating plans, and budgets with the mission priorities and by (re)specifying in each person's *job definition* what specific behaviors and actions are necessary to reflect and achieve the mission. With this approach, responsibility for addressing the hospital's mission priorities no longer becomes the task of only a handful of individuals at the top of the hospital's hierarchy. Rather, responsibility is extended to an army of true believers on the hospital's entire front line.

Of course, any one person's ability to carry out their assigned responsibilities is greatly influenced by their competence and skill to do so. Therefore, all existing hospital employees must be *trained*—or retrained—in a Coordinated fashion to carry out their mission-related responsibilities. You should also seek to secure and Control the behaviors of hospital employees through your hospital's

FIGURE 3

The 'Bart Star' Mission Alignment Model[1]

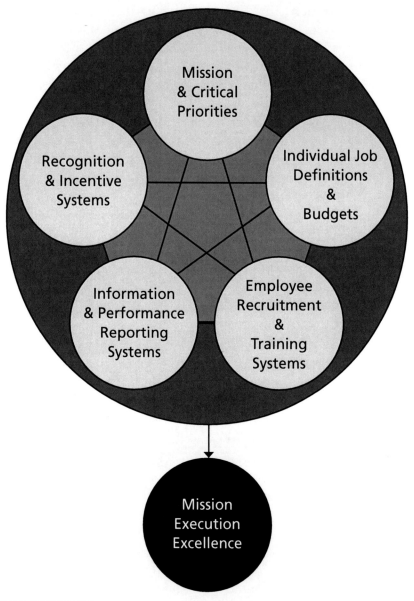

1 Additional information on how to align and execute an organization's complete strategy can be found at: http://CorporateMissionsInc.com

recruitment procedures which should be adjusted to ensure that your hospital only "hires those values" that reinforce the mission.

But none of the actions just listed will matter a hoot *if employees don't care* to do what's required of them in order to execute the mission. Which brings us back once again to the *conundrum* discussed in the Foreword of this book. **So how do you make them care?**

There are two inviolate principles of good management that apply universally in almost every situation. The first is: "**You can't manage what you don't measure.**" What this means in terms of becoming mission-driven is that for every person's assigned responsibility, *a hospital's information system needs to measure and report on how well it is being attended to*. This information is reported both to the individuals concerned as well as to their supervisors. By doing this, you help Control individual action i.e., hospital employees are motivated to correct for any reported discrepancies from agreed-upon mission-related standards of behavior. *Why?* Because when a person has direct and current knowledge of inadequate or unacceptable performance, their sense of individual pride typically prompts them to seek a corrective response. As well, when hospital employees **know** that *their boss knows* whether they are doing a good job or not (i.e., behaving in accordance with the mission), there is no place to hide and so they will work to avoid looking bad, stupid, negligent or dumb.

The second inviolate principle of good management states that: "**what gets rewarded, gets done.**" And so it is imperative that recognition and incentive systems which the hospital has already in place be adjusted to reflect—and Control for—the current priorities stemming from the mission statement. After all, there is nothing more perplexing in a hospital than the folly of expecting X while rewarding Y.

Being mission-driven. It is only when your hospital has followed all of the steps contained in *The 5-C Mission Model* and illustrated in the *Bart Star* that it will become truly mission-driven. Tellingly, the essential ingredient in The Bart Star is *the connecting lines*. By cutting just one or more of these, your hospital increases the probability that its efforts to implement its mission as articulated (as well as the goals and priorities contained therein) will fail.

This is not rocket science. However, becoming mission-driven does require a certain degree of *discipline and mental fortitude* to follow-through on each of the 5-Cs and to *connect all the lines in the Bart Star*. Fortunately, the rewards appear to be worth it! My research over the years has shown time and time again that the organizational performance benefits that come from being truly mission-driven far outweigh the costs, grief and sheer disappointment of not doing do.

In fact, my research demonstrates that **the stronger the "alignment" of ALL organizational systems** (i.e. structure, job descriptions, strategic and operational planning systems, budgeting systems, performance evaluation criteria, the recruitment and training systems, the recognition and incentive systems, and the management information and performance reporting systems) **with a hospital's mission**, the stronger and more significantly positive the correlation is with a **multitude of performance measures** including: satisfaction with the mission statement, the strength of the mission's influence on personal and group behavior, personal commitment to the mission, and satisfaction with the hospital's financial performance. And so, in answer to the burning question **"Does mission matter?"** the answer unequivocally appears to be a resounding **"yes"**.

> *A mission-driven hospital is not nirvana, but it is a vibrant institution in which everyone understands the organization's unique purpose and acts rationally and deliberately in line with it.*

In chapter 4 and the subsequent ones, I'll discuss the research I have conducted in a sample of hospitals and analyze the way in which each of the "5-C"s has contributed to the success or failure of mission in these institutions. Before I present those findings, however, Chapter 3 will provide an overall description of my research and the basis of the operation of the **5-C Mission Model** in the hospitals studied. *(Unless this sort of information really interests you, feel free to skip over it!)*

THREE

Learning About Mission Directly
The Hospital Survey

NOTE: SKIPPING THIS CHAPTER IS OK!

RESEARCH ON MISSION and mission statements can and has followed a number of methods, ranging from direct analyses of organizations' mission statements to *a priori* attempts to synthesize the essence of what mission means. Although this research has provided insights into the components of mission statements, a more scientific approach was used to discern what it is about some mission statements—and the way in which they are promulgated—that makes them so critical to their particular organization.

Research was done to discover:

- what organizations actually included in their mission statements,
- why they wrote them and
- how they went about implementing them.

As well, given the numerous anecdotes about useless and failed mission endeavors, a measure of "satisfaction" was included.

The *healthcare sector* became the focus of this research because it represented an "industry" in which the concept of mission is a natural document, often called for in the course of a hospital's accreditation and one for which research could prove highly beneficial.

While a researcher could use case studies or interviews to gather data, this study used the survey method because it provided the most efficient means for obtaining information on missions in the healthcare sector. Besides efficiency, the survey method allowed my research team to acquire sufficient data to undertake statistical analysis to test, for instance, whether certain items of a hospital's mission content had more impact on its performance *as a 'mission-driven organization'* than others.

Naturally, there are limitations to the approach used (as discussed below). However, we considered the survey method to provide the best overall vehicle for better understanding the importance of mission for the healthcare sector.

PART 1

The Hospital-Survey Process—Four Key Points

1. Asking the Right Questions

A survey document is only as good as the clarity and pertinence of its questions. When a survey is done orally, some misunderstandings about the meaning of questions can be rectified by an astute interviewer. Such attempts at amendment of the survey on the spot, however, can lead to biases in the responses, since the survey instrument could be changed subtly by such interference.

The study's hospital survey was done through the mail, which means the survey instrument itself had to be developed and its questions honed to the point that gave assurance that the proper things were being asked, using the best and most understandable language. The quality and usefulness of the survey findings are therefore dependent on the quality of my questionnaire.

A number of questions were developed to investigate the Creation, Content, Communication, Coordination and Control of hospital mission statements and the processes in which they were undertaken and implemented. The questionnaire was derived from a survey instrument used in earlier research on for-profit firms. To see whether the questionnaire would be comprehensible to respondents, it was successfully pre-tested on a selected group.

2. Selecting and Contacting the Hospitals

The survey was used on Canadian hospitals, all of which, given Canadian public medical insurance, were not-for-profit institutions. A sample of 496 Canadian hospitals that were listed in the *Guide to Canadian Healthcare Facilities* and which were identified as "English-speaking hospitals" having a minimum budget of $2 million each were selected. Excluded were district health organizations (DHOs) as well as hospitals from the French-speaking province of Quebec. DHOs were omitted because they do not perform direct medical procedures but are rather administrative bodies. In regard to Quebec hospitals, the validity of the project could be complicated because of the risk of translation problems inherent in questionnaire development and application.

Of the 496 questionnaires mailed (including one follow-up telephone call), 103 completed questionnaires were returned, which represents a response rate of 20.8 percent.

Table 1 presents some key operating statistics for the hospitals in the sample compared with the characteristics of the remainder of the population. The two groups were compared to determine whether respondents were representative of the Canadian English-speaking hospital population as a whole. It is important in survey research to uncover any potential bias in the respondent population since this can limit generalizations that can be drawn from the research.

TABLE 1: Key Operating Statistics of the Hospitals Studied

	Sample (Mean)	Standard Error of the Sample	Non-response group (Mean)	t-test significance (two-tail) between sample and non-response group
Number of Beds	221	27.5	183	not significant
Number of FTE's	695	104.3	526	not significant
Budget	$52.820	$8.04	$33.435	.023

Table 1 shows there were no significant differences between the sample and the non-respondents either in terms of the number of full-time equivalent employees (FTEs) or beds. The average size of the budget for respondents, however, was significantly greater than that of the rest of the population. This difference in budgetary magnitude means that the findings may not be applicable to hospitals of all sizes. The findings, however, would appear to be valid for larger scale, English-speaking hospitals and perhaps have relevance for similar types of healthcare organizations globally. If that statement is too bold for some, then at least look at the results obtained and **ask yourself: "would this finding apply to my hospital?"** It is argued that your answer will most often times be "yes".

3. The Human Contact in the Survey

The point of contact for the hospitals that received the survey was the *top manager* of the institution, i.e., the CEO/president/executive director/administrator. The top manager was asked to complete the questionnaire or to delegate the task to someone knowledgeable about the hospital's mission statement and its development. Top management was the focus since they should be aware of the mission (if it existed) and also because they were key stakeholders in effecting the success of the mission initiative.

Of the responses received, 61 percent were from the hospital's "top manager" (CEO) while the remainder were all senior-level executives or managers, namely 15 percent vice-president, 14 percent director/manager and 12 percent other. **Because of the differences among the respondents 'ranks' there could be a potential bias arising from "who" specifically responded to the survey and from what organizational level.** A statistical analysis (one-way analysis of variance) was therefore conducted for each of the study's dependent variables (the items in the questionnaire) based on the four categories of respondents (the factor variable). The results showed no significant differences in responses in virtually all cases. Significant differences (at the .05 level or less) in the respondents' answers were found for only two of the variables (i.e., 'the degree of supplier involvement' and 'the degree of influence of the board'). Based on these findings, it was concluded that **there were not sufficient differences among** the answers of the various respondents to warrant a concern with response bias.

4. What About The 79.2% of Hospitals Surveyed That Did Not Respond?

A troubling factor in survey research, especially those done through the mail, is the **possible bias** that can arise because a certain proportion of the population surveyed does not respond. The reasons for not responding can be myriad—lack of interest, lack of time, incorrect addresses or mailing *inter alia*. To have confidence in the findings of the survey, some way was needed to assess the potential for *non-response bias* in the research.

One method of assessing non-response bias would be to compare the characteristics (i.e. of mission development and implementation) of respondents to characteristics of the population. Since this was not possible because of the nature of the research, the non-response bias was evaluated by comparing those who responded to the survey early with those who responded late.

As a stance which is generally accepted, **late repliers are considered more representative of non-respondents than early repliers.** Therefore, the sample was divided into two groups, based on the order in which their completed questionnaires were received. Comparing the two groups, no statistically significant differences in any of the measures were found to warrant concern that late (or non-responders) were in any way different from those anxious to reply. Based on this analysis, it was concluded that **there was no concern for non-response bias in the data.**

PART 2

Analyzing Survey Responses

The hospital survey accomplished more than simply collecting information about what a healthcare institution includes in its mission statement. Indeed, there was interest in the **content** of the mission statement and also the **process** used to develop and promulgate it.

However, it was also important to know whether the content, process and the way in which the mission was applied in day-to-day operations (or not) made a difference to the organization.

Simply finding out the "facts" about mission in hospitals may be interesting, but *understanding the effects of mission on hospital performance* is critical. To do this, a series of statistical analyses were undertaken on the raw data from the survey questionnaires.

The survey results showed that Creation, Content, Communication, Coordination and Control have a significant and distinctive message for hospitals—that each of these factors is important and has special attributes in the hospital sector.

Rather than attempting to summarize the findings at this point, it is sufficient to note that the survey has reinforced the critical nature of mission. From the analysis, **you will clearly see that effective mission statements, applied properly, do affect hospital performance, and affect it positively.** *It's what makes the mission-driven hospital!*

The analysis also made it clear that hospitals have neglected some of their key stakeholders in the mission process in the past, groups that must (or should) contribute to the ongoing success of healthcare institutions. These and other findings, along with the specific research questions addressed, will be discussed in more detail in the remainder of the book.

It is imperative, however, to realize that the findings are based on the survey described above and are only as valid as the methods deployed to undertake this research. Some of the potential limitations of the research include:

- Were the right questions asked and were they comprehensible?
- Were the right people asked and were they knowledgeable and honest?
- Did those who responded represent an unusual or biased group or are they representative?

Caution was exercised by trying to minimize biases and test for their presence. However, no research can claim 100 percent certainty in its results. Just as medical doctors cannot assure their patients of an absolutely certain cure, absolute claims about the survey results cannot be made.

Despite limitations, however, there is confidence in the conclusions about hospital mission statements drawn from the survey. And feedback from articles, talks and workshops with hospitals have confirmed the belief that these findings offer important lessons on mission for the entire healthcare sector—not just nationally, but globally as well.

FOUR

Creation
How Hospitals Effectively Develop their Mission

PART 1

The Research

It should be acknowledged as a truism that little attention has been given by previous researchers to the actual *process* used to develop and implement mission statements. Moreover, traditional commentary on why and how missions are created has largely been only normative or prescriptive in nature. My examination of previous writings has determined that there are at least ten reasons for why an organization might want to consider developing a mission statement in the first place. These include:

- To motivate/inspire organization members
- To define the organization's scope of operations/activities
- To enable top managers (especially the CEO) to assert greater authority over the firm's activities
- To provide a basis for allocating resources in a more focused manner

- To ensure that the interests of external stakeholders (e.g., government, customers, suppliers) are not ignored
- To create standards of behavior for the organization's members
- To provide common direction/unity of purpose transcending individual and departmental needs
- To enable employees to identify with the organization's purpose/direction and to encourage those who do not to leave
- To promote a strong corporate culture (i.e., shared values)
- To refocus the organization during a crisis

None of these is mutually exclusive. However, very little evidence has been gathered indicating which rationales may be more useful or important for driving performance or whether some rationales are more successful than others in achieving their stated aims. Only recently have mission rationales and their impact on subsequent performance been explicitly considered.

In one of my own works, for instance, I studied the affect of the 10 "mission drivers" (or rationales) listed above on selected measures of organizational performance (4 financial, 1 behavioral) in 75 large advanced-technology firms. I repeated the study a few years later, only this time looking at large industrial firms. A significant observation I drew from the results of both research investigations was that while mission rationales did not appear to have any serious effect on financial performance, *many of the mission drivers showed a significant impact in terms of their ability to positively influence employee behavior.* Moreover, the high 'behavior influencing' drivers were not the same in each study. *Different mission drivers were being used—or favoured—by different types of organizations.* These observations were later confirmed in still yet another of my studies looking at mission rationales in innovative and non-innovative firms.

From these observations, it seemed logical to conclude that mission statements, including both their rationales and their *formulation processes*, could be substantially different for organizations in the non-for-profit (NFP) sector, especially hospitals. After all, if different types of for-profit firms have different reasons for why they undertake missions, should not hospitals in the not-for-profit sector likewise have distinguishing rationales behind their mission efforts?

Interestingly, one of the major variables of interest in prior studies concerning *the mission creation process* appears to be *the number and type of stakeholders* who need to be involved or engaged. Previous findings have suggested that there are up to nine stakeholder groups whose participation in developing the mission could be considered important. These include:

- The CEO
- Senior managers
- Middle managers
- Non-managers (front-line workers)
- Consultants
- Shareholders (i.e., owners, or the funding government)
- Customers (or Patients-Clients)
- Suppliers
- Board of Directors

The main reason for wanting and encouraging their participation is the conventional managerial wisdom which argues that involvement in the development of almost anything (such as a budget or a policy) will motivate participants to greater "buy-in", cause them to work harder to achieve it (thereby affecting their behavior) and create more satisfaction in their work. And while no one has ever proved a conclusive causal link between participation, motivation and behavior, the centrality of participation as a management tool for creating goal congruity is ubiquitous. We all believe intuitively there is such a link.

My own research has also contributed to the continuation of this line of thinking. For instance, in two of my early studies, I found that broad participation by a large range of internal stakeholder groups in the mission-development process was significantly and positively correlated with various performance outcomes.

In terms of the current study, I hoped that by identifying those mission creation processes which were not only 'most favoured' but also ones which enhanced performance, I'd be able to help better guide hospitals in their *quest to become mission-driven*. And that quest begins with <u>C</u>reation, the first C of my 5-C model.

PART 2

Creation and the Hospital Survey

Research Questions

To determine what type of *mission creation process* was most effective in the hospitals participating in the study, we focused on several areas:

- What are the *primary 'drivers' or 'rationales'* for developing a mission statement in an NFP hospital? Are some rationales used more often than others?
- To what extent are *various stakeholders involved* in the creation of a hospital's mission? How much influence does each stakeholder group have over the development of their hospital's mission?
- What types of 'development styles' are used in the creation of a hospital's mission statement?
- What impact do different mission creation processes have on hospital outcomes and performance, if any? Are some processes more important/useful than others?

Outcome/Performance Relationships With Rationale

As in my earlier studies, I used a number of outcome measures to assess the impact of 'mission drivers' and 'mission participation' on hospital performance—and ultimately as a proxy for assessing the degree to which a hospital was mission-driven. Outcome measures were selectively defined as:

- The degree of satisfaction with the overall process used to develop the current mission statement
- The degree of satisfaction with the current mission statement
- The extent to which the mission statement influenced the behavior of the respondent
- The extent to which the mission was a source of energy
- The extent to which the mission was a guide for day-to-day decision making

- The extent to which the mission statement appeared to influence the behavior of members throughout the organization
- The degree to which hospital members were committed to the mission statement
- The degree of satisfaction with the hospital's overall financial performance

Hospital administrators were asked to rate each of these performance measures on a 10-point scale, where 0 = not at all, and 9 = to the greatest possible extent.

An Aside On "Outcome Measures"

Though some readers may be troubled by the way in which performance outcomes were "measured," I proceeded in this manner for good reasons. For example, the *satisfaction-with-overall-financial-performance measure* attempts to assess bottom-line financial results. I could have independently collected measures of financial performance, such as profitability or revenues, but traditional indicators like these are not considered appropriate performance measures for NFP organizations in general and hospitals in particular. Indeed, it is extremely difficult to compare the financial performance of NFP organizations because of their different operating structures and underlying social-welfare purposes. To assess NFPs by their bottom lines, as I did with for-profit firms, disregards and underrates the more subtle underlying objectives of their existence.

In addition to this problem of making sense of NFP numbers, some researchers believe that numerical performance measures are themselves open to many interpretations and that there are too many other considerations to be accounted for and controlled (e.g., time, industry, size, overall strategy) to use these numbers in isolation. *Managers' perceptions of success, on the other hand, generally take many, if not most, of these variables into consideration.* In fact, I can argue that it is managers' perceptions that ultimately control their behavior, not the numbers.

Numbers by themselves are also meaningless without context: for example, a firm's reduction of its expenses by 10% may not mean much if others in the industry achieved greater expense decreases or if other important internal measures like loyalty and motivation declined in tandem. Likewise, increasing revenues by 50% could be spectacular in some cases but not when industry sales have expanded by 100%!

My experience has been that managers automatically take into account these broader considerations when asked to evaluate performance in perceptual or scaled terms. Accordingly, this is the way in which I approached hospitals' financial performance: *the satisfaction managers had with their hospital's financial situation is a reliable measure of performance given that they are the ones with the best familiarity of their organization's relative financial standing.*

PART 3

Why Hospitals Decide to Create a Mission and the Process They Use to Formulate it

Popularity of the Mission Rationales

Of the 10 identified reasons for wanting to create a mission statement in the first place, it was found that seven were utilized by the participating hospitals to a more significant degree than others. They are (in descending order):

- To provide a common purpose
- To define the scope of the hospital's activities
- To promote shared values
- To motivate/inspire hospital employees
- To set behavior standards
- To enable employees to identify with the hospital
- To address needs of external stakeholders

Three of these rationales—'common purpose', 'defining scope' and 'promoting shared values'—were rated by hospital leaders as their dominant driver (my highest rating) in at least 50% of the cases. In contrast, 'enabling the CEO to assert control', 'refocusing the organization during crisis', and 'providing a basis of resource allocation' were the rationales observed to be not used to any significant extent.

Interestingly, the rationales most frequently employed by the hospital managers were similar to those used by the top managers in my study of mission statements in selected industrial firms. However, **the intensity** with which these primary mission drivers were used in the current study was much higher than the scores obtained for the industrial for-profit managers.

Do Some Rationales Make More of a Difference to Success than Others?

Five of the ten mission rationales were found to be significantly and positively correlated with the performance measures. They are (in order):

- To motivate/inspire hospital employees
- To promote shared values
- To provide a common purpose
- To guide resource allocation
- To ensure that the interests of external stakeholders are not ignored

These results suggest that certain mission rationales are more broadly associated with success and performance than others. Consequently, hospital managers should be more cognizant of these performance-driven rationales when they contemplate the basis of their next mission formulation/re-evaluation process.

Are Some Mission Rationales More Achievable than Others?

As part of this study, the hospital administrators were also asked to rate the degree to which they believed the aims and aspirations contained in their stated mission rationales were actually being achieved. Notwithstanding the strong frequency of use for the seven mission drivers identified above, it was surprising that the most *infrequently used* mission rationale (i.e., 'allocating resources') was the strongest among users in terms of its rated "achievement". What this suggests is that those hospital managers not making use of this rationale may not be taking full advantage of the one that provides the "best" or the "shortest" route to *success with their mission*. After all, *the way in which an NFP allocates its scarce resources is typically considered to be the most recognizable manifestation—and tangible expression—of its strategy and associated mission.* Thus, hospital managers would be well served to consider *resource allocation* (via strategic and operational plans and budgets) as a primary motivator when they create or revisit their mission statement.

In contrast, 'defining a common purpose' and 'creating shared-values' were found to be the highest mentioned mission rationales in this study but they were also ones that received lowest ratings in terms of their perceived achievement. The popularity of these two drivers is not surprising given that they are classic rationales from the mission literature.

The low achievement of these two "core" mission rationales, however, raises an important red flag for hospital managers: trying to create shared values or a common purpose is not an easy goal (or, at least, not as easy in comparison to some other mission drivers such as 'developing a mission for more effective resource allocation'). Moreover, most of the mission statements in this study were recent creations (within the last five years). This would suggest, therefore, that managers may need to allow sufficient time to achieve some of the more challenging aspirations underlying their missions, a length of time which our sample had not yet passed.

In other words, for some mission rationales, the more unrealistic the manager's expectations for mission delivery, the more he/she will be frustrated by the mission itself. There are no 10-minute-manager-style shortcuts, no speedy ways for organizations to create a common direction or to adopt a widely held set of organizational values. These are important and powerful organizational initiatives but they are fraught with difficulties, setbacks, disappointments and resistance.

However, the payoff from harnessing the potential of these two particular mission drivers is enormous! They were among the top three rationales (the third being "to motivate/inspire hospital members") correlating most strongly with all of the performance outcome measures. Expending the time and energy to bring these drivers to fruition, therefore, appears to be worth the effort.

Organizational Scope: Popular and Achievable, but Low-Performance Impact

'Defining the *scope* of a hospital's business/operations' was found, as a mission driver, to be both very popular and relatively easy to achieve. Yet it was also observed to have a weaker impact on performance than almost all of the others, illustrating that just because something is easy to do does not necessarily mean it is rewarding. So it was not a surprise that the scope driver had such high-usage frequency given the near obsession of the strategy literature with the concept and the need to answer the question "what business(es) are we in?"

But the rationale's lack of impact on performance was also interesting: it seems to indicate that perhaps hospital managers should spend less time fretting over business definitions and, instead, focus their efforts on activities that appear to offer a higher return on their most valuable investment resource—their time. While defining the scope of the hospital's operations is important, it may be best left to other occasions and to strategic documents other than the mission statement.

Ineffective Mission Drivers: *Crisis and CEO Control*

The *'to-refocus-the-organization-in-a-crisis'* driver also produced some interesting relationships: low usage frequency, relatively easy achievement *and low impact on performance*. This suggests that when missions are created for the purpose of refocusing the organization in a crisis, the act of refocusing is usually and successfully achieved. But, paradoxically, the driver does not lead to high performance on any of our outcome measures. In other words, the road to high performance nirvana in the middle of some organizational crisis does not appear to be paved with a mission statement. And managers that attempt to use one to solve an emergency or divert disaster will be repaid poorly for their efforts. Hence their low use! Instead, wise managers should seek to deploy a mission statement in other situations for which the payoffs are higher and more secure.

Interestingly, the least important motivation or rationale for hospital managers to undertake the creation of a mission statement was "*to give their CEO more control over the organization.*" The degree of success hospitals had with the driver was low; and the impact of the rationale on hospital performance was negligible. Thus, hospital managers should avoid using a mission statement for this purpose, or only do so at their peril.

Stakeholder Involvement and Influence

Considerable variability was found to exist in the *frequency* with which various stakeholder groups were included in the mission-development process. Not surprisingly, the mission-development process at the various hospitals seems to have been restricted largely to internal stakeholders. The process was dominated by both upper-level managers and the hospital's board of directors (with middle and non-managers (the front line) involved only to a moderate degree)— a finding consistent with my earlier study of leading North American corporations. It is also consistent with the conventional mission statement literature which suggests that the development of a mission by the board and top management can promote *goal congruence*. But, as noted earlier, the factors of frequency and influence alone are not indicative of "best practice." To try to understand whose participation in mission development matters, it was necessary to look at which groups had an impact on hospital performance and contributed to a hospital becoming mission-driven.

Stakeholder Involvement and Performance: Which Stakeholders Should Hospitals Involve In Mission Development?

Further investigation showed that the involvement of some stakeholder groups appears to have a greater/lesser impact on hospital performance than others and that only five of the nine stakeholder groups (i.e. patients-clients; senior managers; shareholders/funding government; middle managers; and front line workers) had a significantly positive impact on hospital performance.

Also, given both the high frequency of involvement and influence of the CEO and board of directors, it was somewhat surprising that their participation was not observed to affect hospital performance other than in a very limited fashion.

This research, therefore, offers new insight on the necessity of giving involvement in the mission development process to *many* stakeholder groups *but especially those that may have been previously overlooked or undervalued.* For example, it would be difficult to imagine a mission process that does not involve the CEO. Yet the survey results here suggest that the involvement of many other groups is actually more important than the CEO in relation to performance outcomes. This is not to argue that CEO involvement in mission development is not necessary for improved performance, but it does suggest that the CEO does need to be joined by many others in the hospital.

More importantly, there is a "moral" lesson here for hospital administrators: by excluding certain stakeholders from a hospital's mission statement development, they sacrifice some unique opportunities to enhance performance and become mission-driven. For example, involving senior managers, middle managers, front line workers, and especially patients-clients in the creation of a hospital's mission statement was found to have a significantly positive relationship with performance. Yet, with the exception of senior managers, these groups were not well represented in most mission development exercises. Possibly, the exclusion of these groups is a matter of administrative convenience—saving time in the development of the mission and not being confronted with the "messy" necessity of reaching a consensus from the multiple perspectives these groups would bring to the process. Or, it may simply be that administrators are unaware of the performance benefits associated with involving certain groups of stakeholders. Hopefully, with the publication of this book, that will no longer be the case—or the excuse!

Mission Quality: Synthesizing Many Ideas Into One Mission, One Collective Focus

Another major reason for having broad involvement by hospital stakeholders in the mission creation process lies in the nature of the limited stakeholder knowledge which senior hospital administrators generally possess. Even though they may be very well versed in their particular areas of expertise, they are typically not aware of the needs and beliefs of other stakeholder groups. So, it would appear that to achieve the broadest understanding necessary to create a workable, meaningful mission statement, it is vital that hospital executives actively seek participation from these underrepresented groups in their mission-development process.

But it's even more than just getting the mission "right". Broadening participation (by just asking for *feedback* on various mission statement *drafts*) also instils "ownership" and acceptance of the mission in stakeholders. And ownership or empowerment means that various stakeholders (especially employees at the front line) may be *inspired* to act according to the mission and more dedicated to its achievement.

The strategy-formulation literature has long argued that a high amount of stakeholder participation is typically related to higher levels of employee performance. Since the mission development process is a seminal event in strategic planning, it was not that surprising to discover that a similar participation/performance link also occurred in our hospital sample. In particular, it was observed that *higher levels of participation by almost all hospital stakeholder groups contributed to better hospital performance.* (This is also consistent with an earlier study of mine looking at for-profit firms.)

But there is also another aspect of wide stakeholder participation driving performance. Hospitals are diverse organizations comprised of individuals with many different points of view. Finding ways to bring their diverse ideas into the mission development process helps to identify commonalities and allows the mission statement to encapsulate the vital perspectives of all constituencies. Indeed, it was found that by increasing the "total involvement" of all hospital stakeholders in mission development created the ideal environment for hospital employees to become highly "energized" and "influenced" by the mission. This is because when hospital employees see large numbers of other stakeholders—both internal *and* external—involved in their hospital's mission development, they typically feel there is widespread support and commitment to it. This, in turn, makes it more likely that the mission statement will be treated as a "real" and "live" document to guide and inspire—as opposed to one that has been drafted by a handful of senior managers (perhaps with the board) at an expensive weekend retreat.

Finally, there was one interesting difference between the responses of the hospital administrators reported here and an earlier study of mine concerning for-profit managers. In the not-for-profit/hospital setting, 'shareholder/funder involvement' correlated significantly with 'mission-process satisfaction' while CEO involvement did not. The reverse occurred in the for-profit study. A major reason why the hospitals' respondents saw shareholder/funder involvement as more important than the CEO's may arise from the fact that governments (as shareholders) have assumed a wider mandate and taken a more active role in monitoring the public hospital system than typically occurs in the for-profit sector. This study's sample of hospital administrators came from large, publicly funded institutions which recognize that governments have to serve 'the public good'. Shareholders of for-profit companies generally act as economic rationalists and maximizing returns is their dominant concern, not social welfare.

Process Style: Does It Matter?

Just as soliciting broad stakeholder participation is considered important for effective mission development, the current study thought it important to question hospital managers about the type of *process style* used to develop their missions. After all, if a hospital's style of mission development is found lacking, its stakeholders will withdraw their participation. Participants were therefore asked to **rate the extent to which their organization's mission development process was:**

- Autocratic/top-down
- Flexible (i.e., not formally prescribed)
- Simple (i.e., not many steps)
- Creative (i.e., unique to the organization/not copied from a textbook)

Interestingly, the results showed that the *style* with which the mission statement is developed is integral to success.

Of the four types of *process styles* used in creating their missions, most hospitals appeared to want to avoid a "top-down/autocratic" process. Instead, they preferred one that is "flexible", "simple" and "creative". Additionally, only three styles were found to have a significant impact on performance: creative and flexible processes had a positive impact while the top-down/autocratic process had a negative influence on all performance indicators.

This research, therefore, offers a number of insights into what the characteristics of a successful mission development process for hospitals should be. First, the process clearly should not be an autocratic or top-down exercise in which the hospital CEO and the top executives simply dictate the mission. Rather, it should be one in which various members from all parts of the hospital share their viewpoints and resolve their disagreements so as to design a unique and enduring mission statement. Also, as previously discussed, the more hospital stakeholders there are who can lead and advance the process, the better.

A second insight is that a hospital's mission process should not be rigid and formal. Instead, mission architects should be allowed to take whatever steps necessary to arrive at a suitable final product. This means avoiding a rigid timetable for completing the mission since it is only when stakeholders have given broad agreement and support to one that the process is finished. Indeed, Jack Welch, now retired CEO of General Electric, claims that it took almost three years to formulate and finalize GE's mission statement.

A third insight is that an effective hospital mission formulation process needs to be a creative one. Therefore, rather than strictly following a particular textbook's mission "rubric," a hospital may be better served by developing its own "homemade" or original process. After all, the local hospital managers *should* know what sort of mission process suits their environment best. This, of course, does not mean that they should not seek outside expertise and counsel—they just don't need to be slavishly or *automatonically* hidebound to it.

Finally, it was discovered that a simple mission development process is not necessarily the most successful. In fact, sacrificing simplicity may be the price which hospital administrators must pay to get the more consistent and robust payoffs from the other process-style variables: creativity, flexibility and broad participation. By making their hospital's mission-development process one that is democratic, flexible and creative—style variables that have clear performance benefits—simplicity may need to be compromised. Indeed, the desire for mission success—and becoming truly mission-driven— makes the choice clear.

So overall, the manner in which a mission statement is developed and the "process style" used are important considerations in the Creation of a hospital's mission.

PART 4

Some Final Thoughts On The First "C"

Defining an appropriate mission development process is central to the Creation of mission statements—the mover and driver of getting a mission statement's development off the ground. Appropriate mission rationales, though, are not, as we have seen, the most frequently cited ones nor the ones that can be successfully achieved with ease. Sometimes appropriate mission drivers are difficult to achieve in short order. The same holds true for the choice of participants to help formulate the mission and the administrative style which overrides the process. In fact, the insights discovered here seem counter intuitive: that the front line may have as much or more to say about a hospital's strategic mission as those in the executive suite and that simplicity in the formulation process may not always be to the organization's advantage. And finally, having a mission for its own sake is not worth the effort unless there is some expectation of a performance payoff. Accordingly, what all of this means is that hospital managers must look at their mission creation process carefully, thoughtfully and thoroughly. It is the essential—and critical—first step in developing the mission-driven hospital.

A MINI "MISSION CREATION" CASE EXAMPLE

Background

St. Jude's Villa (SJV) has a long and distinguished history as one of the largest long-term-care (LTC) service providers for seniors in its area. In 1884, the Sisters of St. Jude accepted the responsibility for providing care for the elderly and disadvantaged from the local Roman Catholic Diocese. By 2012, SJV not only had a 370+ bed facility (recently renovated and renewed) but also had life equity-condominiums as well as rental apartments for younger, still independent seniors.

SJV is recognized throughout the LTC community for its innovative, quality resident care in a comfortable, aesthetically pleasing, home-like environment.

SJV's success is linked intrinsically to its development and dedication to its mission and values. Indeed, mission is so deeply engrained in SJV's culture that it forms the basis for all planning and operations over both the long and short-term. The *sense of mission* that pervades the organization can be traced back to 1879, when the founders grounded their new establishment in the Christian values of their order (e.g., respect, service, charity and dignity). These values became the basis in 1988 when, after 104 years of service, SJV created and displayed its first formal mission statement on its Board-room wall, a statement which reflected the faith-based, values-driven mission and organizational philosophy developed by the Sisters of St. Jude.

Mission Creation at St. Jude's Villa

Mission at SJV has undergone a number of reviews and validations since its first formal writing. In 1993, the CEO was charged with the task of leading SJV into fiscal solvency (over three previous years the deficit had escalated greatly). As it happened, the CEO's embrace of the mission played a vital role in the successful reorganization of SJV and the consequent return to financial solvency. By imbuing his management and planning with the belief that a mission's ethical and moral standards *must* govern actions and decisions, he rallied employees and made SJV a markedly more efficient and effective organization.

In 1997, following SJV's return to financial health, the CEO sensed the need to review and possibly revise the Villa's mission statement. The mission he inherited was over four pages long! He then asked his vice-president of Planning and Support Services to lead the mission renewal project. This project took 14 months to complete, involved considerable consultation with a wide range of stakeholders and eventually resulted in a new, one-page mission. As well, a process was formally established to regularly review the mission statement and related documents for consistency and relevance.

Since the 1997 revision, the mission has been reviewed several times using a process involving extensive surveys and meetings with various stakeholders. In particular, *all Board members, all staff and numerous clients* are asked to review the mission statement and indicate whether SJV is living up to its aspirations and organizational values. The SJV mission is then compared with the mission of SJV's "parent organization" to ensure that the two continue to be compatible and complementary. Each revision is approved by the Mission Governing Committee of the Board of Directors and becomes the basis of the next strategic plan.

The process to craft, consult and accept each iteration of the mission statement takes several months. The slow pace, though, is deliberate. The CEO strongly believes that when it comes to developing mission/vision/values (MVV), sufficient time must be taken to do the job right the first time and that people affected by it must be involved if management wants their buy-in.

SJV's rationale for creating its mission, vision and related documents has been a strong one: to pull the organization together behind a rallying message—*LOVE, or "Living Our Values Everyday."* Besides this powerful rationale, SJV's mission is developed and re-newed from an inclusive, participatory process that draws widely from the thoughts and opinions of multiple stakeholders. SJV uses a bottom-up, wide-ranging, creative process that builds in the time necessary to assess a broad sample of constituents and they actively listen to dissension. Because the process has been so consultative, SJV's constituents continue to be very aware of their mission (with over 95% of respondents saying so in a recent survey). They also claim to be largely satisfied with and committed to it. Thus, while SJV has revisited its mission many times over the years, the longevity of its *core values-based message* has helped to make the mission integral and meaningful throughout the entire organization.

FIVE

Content

The Ingredients of a Successful Mission
Statement

THERE ARE NUMEROUS ITEMS that could be included in a hospital mission statement, but only some which make a difference to hospital performance. My hospital research has shown that, as with rationales for creating a mission, certain content is chosen more often than others (because of their supposed popularity or perceived attainability) while unknowledgeable of the fact that some content is more effective in changing behavior and improving performance outcomes.

It would be nice if I could prescribe a "fill in the blanks" hospital mission statement like the legal-will kits sold at stationery stores, but that would not help you at all if the goal is to develop content that will positively affect behavior—*a key to becoming mission-driven*—in your institution. Good, effective mission Content can only come from understanding the unique nature of your own hospital's activity and aspirations.

PART 1

Mission Content and the Hospital Survey

Because of the lack of study of mission content issues in the health-care sector, my survey was designed to investigate three questions:

- What are the specific content characteristics of mission statements in hospitals?
- Does the inclusion of a particular mission statement component appear to make a difference in terms of hospital performance outcome measures?
- Does the quality with which a particular mission component is *articulated or stated* in the mission statement impact performance outcome measures, if at all?

To find answers, I used an inventory of 22 components that I and other researchers had previously identified as potentially being part of a mission statement (See Exhibit 1 in Chapter 1). The next step was to include in the survey a set of questions asking participants to indicate the extent to which each of the components was mentioned in their hospital's mission statement.

Besides this straightforward count of what their hospital mission statements did or did not contain, I also asked respondents to indicate their *level of satisfaction with 'how well' each of the content items was written into their hospital's mission statement.*

PART 2

The Analysis

Popular Vs. Unpopular Mission Content

Hospital administrators do indeed have distinct preferences as to which items they wish to include in their organization's mission statement. Six items proved to be most popular and clearly specified:

- Statement of purpose
- Statement of values/beliefs
- One clear compelling goal
- Specification of patients-clients served
- Specification of services/products offered
- Concern for satisfying patients/clients

The finding that 'specific patients-clients served' and 'services/products offered' were high-use items is particularly interesting because my research and that of others have observed that neither of these two components is typically found in for-profit mission statements. For healthcare operations, however, the trend toward managed-care models is causing many hospitals to narrow their scope of operations and specify target populations. Thus, it is becoming increasingly necessary for hospitals to include more precise definitions of their operations (i.e., services, patients, uniqueness) in their mission statements. And as budgetary cuts and hospital closures become more prevalent, it is possible that healthcare institutions that do not serve a unique purpose will be more susceptible to closure than others.

At the same time, if popularity alone was the decisive criterion for including an item in a hospital's mission statement then 'low mentioned' mission content items such as 'desired competitive position', 'competitive strategy' and 'concern for shareholders/owners/funders' would be non-starters. Yet, from the point of view of the managed-care models that are becoming ever more prevalent, healthcare administrators may be ill advised to ignore the need to become more competitive and to not seriously consider possibly noting these items in their stated mission.

One of the major conclusions that I gleaned from the survey results, however, is that popularity is neither a necessary nor sufficient reason for a hospital to include a specific item of content in its mission statement. And as you will now see, a strong positive relationship between content and performance is the more potent argument for including an item than whether it was mentioned the most times in a sample of hospital mission statements.

Choosing Mission Content To Guide Performance

I discovered that several important and significant relationships exist between only *some* of the 22 mission statement components examined and the performance outcome measures used to determine the degree to which a hospital is mission-driven. My findings demonstrate comprehensively and conclusively *that high quality mission content and hospital performance are linked* and, surprisingly *that performance outcomes do not always arise from the most popular content.* The mission content items most important for achieving the highest levels of hospital performance and becoming mission-driven are:

- *distinctive competence* (*)
- specification of patients-clients served
- specification of services/products offered
- *unique identity* (*)[1]
- concern for satisfying patient-clients
- *concern for satisfying employees* (*)
- *concern for society* (*)
- *concern for shareholders/owners/funders* (*)

(*)—indicates that the item was NOT a high frequency-of-mention mission content item

Additionally, one of the major messages I have for hospital administrators is that expressing a concern for satisfying each of the four major hospital stakeholder groups (i.e., patients-clients, employees, society and shareholders) is a crucial aspect of achieving *'effective' mission content.* Indeed, each of these expressions of stakeholder concern was found to be significantly related to the various performance outcome measures including *high levels of satisfaction reported regarding the resultant mission statement.*

As a result of these findings, hospital leaders and their mission development teams now have greater guidance—rooted in best practice and not just popular practice—that can better facilitate the design

---

1 NOTE: As long as key stakeholders (but, especially employees) feel that their hospital's mission statement is unique and can explain specifically how it is different from those of others, then it meets the test of "uniqueness".

of 'highly effective' mission statements for their organizations. They now know which mission statement components seem to really matter (i.e. that have the greatest or far reaching performance impact) and can use that knowledge in their consultation dialogue with various stakeholder groups and individuals-of-influence.

By now, though, I hope that you also appreciate how dangerous it is to rely on simple frequency counts (as indicators of what other hospitals are doing) to determine what content to include or exclude in your hospital's mission statement. Indeed, the rather mindless exercise of "following the crowd" when designing a mission statement may be part of the reason why many hospital managers view missions as ineffective and simply "motherhood" statements. My results show that popularity is both misleading and risky if you wish to become (more) mission-driven by means of the exercise.

I am frequently asked, however, why the inclusion of a hospital's financial objectives was not found to be an effective practice? I believe that the reason for this stems primarily from the general nature and purpose of mission statements versus that of objectives. Conventional wisdom suggests that mission statements should be somewhat general, yet organizationally identifiable, statements of purpose, direction and focus. Objectives, on the other hand, are highly specific and detailed and normally attached to a time frame.

It is, of course, essential for managers to ultimately specify numbers that "quantify" their organization's mission focus because they help hospital employees monitor their progress against the mission itself. (As you will see in a later chapter, coordination of hospital objectives with the mission statement is critical to achieving high performance.) However, financial measures can be a turnoff in a hospital's mission statement which is intended to be more aspirational *and* inspirational. Hospital managers are therefore wise to include them someplace else—as my survey results have shown that they have been.

Quality Content And Performance

This chapter has been focused on trying to delineate what is popular versus what matters in the content of a hospital's mission statement. I now want to take this one step further. When I analyzed the relationship between *how well* a mission content item is expressed and its relationship to our performance outcome measures of mission-driven-ness, I found another source of positive performance impact affecting almost every mission item. In other words, *not any wording for a mission statement component will necessarily do. Or, put another way—quality matters! And, if it is ignored, it could even send the wrong signal.*

Take, for instance, the mission component of "concern for employees". If hospital associates are not highly satisfied with how well their organization's 'concern for employees' is expressed in the mission, it might appear to them that the item was simply "thrown in" out of convention rather than trying to articulate *thoughtfully and sincerely* the importance of employees to the institution. Employees, in turn, might interpret this as a lack of "real" concern and, therefore, feel uninspired to follow the mission as it relates to other stakeholders. Spending the time to express "concern for employees" in a quality manner thus appears to be important. One example of poorly articulating this mission component would be as follows:

"Hospital X encourages its staff, including medical staff, to maintain a high level of competency and provide quality care to the extent of its resources. The hospital also recognizes the value of the contribution of the Hospital Auxiliary and other volunteers."

This is a poorly expressed statement because it puts the role of employees as "quasi-machines" whose sole function is "to produce" i.e., to provide a service of some kind to others. Their "value" is recognized as a sort of afterthought.

In contrast, an example of an extremely satisfactory expression of 'concern for employees' might be:

"At Hospital X, we foster an environment of mutual respect that recognizes the value of our staff and volunteers. We promise to treat each other with courtesy and cheerfulness. We aim especially to bring personal fulfillment and meaning to the lives of all our associates—regardless of the position they hold in our organization."

This statement is outstanding because it shows the high value which the hospital places on its associates as equal stakeholders—second to none. Their personal interests, growth and fulfillment matter.

Hospital administrators should, therefore, pay particular attention to the quality with which certain mission statement components are written (especially the performance enhancing ones) when formulating (or re-formulating) their organization's mission statement. (We will look at this issue again when we discuss a clear expression of mission as part of the third "<u>C</u>": <u>C</u>ommunication.)

PART 3

Parting Wisdom on Mission Content

Everyone in a hospital has ideas (some good, some bad) of what should be included in a mission statement. For healthcare organizations in particular, though, the content of mission seems obvious, from its dedication to serving its patients-clients to a view of its unique role in society. What is not so obvious is some of those other items of potential mission content, such as distinctive competence or desired competitive position. For many healthcare administrators these concepts smack too much of the for-profit, cut-throat business world. Yet, as we have seen, these items of mission content (as well as others) are significantly related to the performance outcomes for the hospital and have an important contribution to making the institution become mission-driven.

Moreover, while convention and tradition would have us include certain items in a mission statement, not all of these items are equally important. This research has shown that some mission components appear to matter more than others when it comes to their relationship with performance outcomes. And those that matter, may not always be the most popular.

Finally, the newly discovered relationship between the quality of expression in a mission's content and hospital performance is an important consideration in trying to define what matters in a mission statement. Presenting the mission in an articulate, well-thought-out manner significantly affects the degree to which the mission is embraced. Thus, *what we say, how we say it and what our aims are— all affect mission success.* Hospital administrators should, therefore, take great care to be clear and passionate when formulating the truly important—and essential—components of their hospital's mission statement.

A MINI "MISSION CONTENT" CASE EXAMPLE

Background

Sunnyvale Metropolitan Hospital (SMH) has been a fixture in its city for over 118 years. Established in 1892, SMH has become a premier research and teaching hospital affiliated with a major local university. It is one of the largest hospitals in North America and provides the designated adult trauma centre for all of its downtown inhabitants. SMH employs over 5,000 employees, supervises in excess of 500 in-patient beds and operates extensive outpatient clinics.

Content

An analysis of SMH's current mission Content (see **Exhibit** 3) shows that it successfully addresses all the critical 'components' which were shown in this Chapter to be important for inclusion in a hospital's mission statement. It masterfully defines the hospital's identity and *raison d'être* thereby providing a comprehensive, all-encompassing view of what the organization is and what it stands for. From **Exhibit** 3 one can readily see that the mission:

- Recognizes its history and tradition of care
- Concerns itself with patients, their worth and dignity as well as with its staff, valuing and respecting them and allowing for growth
- Realizes that patient care is holistic care (i.e., exemplary physical, emotional and spiritual care for patients and family)
- Includes its commitment to social, educational, environmental and community service and responsibility
- Focuses on quality and excellence and a recognition of the tradition of caring, which is part of SMH's history

As well, the mission cites three critical priorities for SMH: academic excellence; operating as a values-driven organization; and recognizing the uniqueness of SMH in providing healthcare to all who seek it, especially underprivileged inner-city dwellers.

Indeed, SMH's modern mission is based on a longstanding "grand inspiration"—*altruistic care of the poor and downtrodden who need medical care*. As such, the mission is designed to motivate staff to make decisions and conduct themselves in line with the organization's noble and selfless traditions and values. But it also has the added benefit of helping to give SMH a renewed understanding of itself, where it came from, what it stands for today and where and how goals will be accomplished.

The Content of SMH's mission is therefore very inclusive of the way in which the hospital views itself and the way in which it believes it should operate. Indeed, the Content is representative of what I argued in Chapter 4 needs to be in a mission statement. The only negative that could be attributed to it, is its length, which makes it difficult to memorize. But, because the statement contains everything SMH believes to be necessary to characterize its mission and values, length may not be an issue at all. In fact, because there is so much specific direction, it makes the Mission more actionable, particularly for managers and front-line workers.

Exhibit 3

Sunnyvale Metropolitan Hospital's Mission Statement

Specific products/ services offered

Unique identity

Sunnyvale Metropolitan Hospital is an academic health-care provider, fully affiliated with Sunnyvale University and committed to innovative patient care, teaching and research. Established in 1893, Sunnyvale remains dedicated to treating all with respect, compassion, and dignity.

Concern for patients

At Sunnyvale Metropolitan Hospital, we are guided by our recognition of the worth of each person and by our commitment to excellence and leadership by:

Distinctive competence

Specific products/ services offered

- Providing exemplary physical, emotional, and spiritual care for each person we serve

Unique identity

- Balancing a continuing commitment to the care of the poor and those most in need with the provision of highly specialized services to a broader community

Concern for patients

Specific products/ services offered

- Building a work environment where each person is valued, respected and has an opportunity for personal and professional growth

Specific products/ services offered

Concern for employees

- Striving for the advancement of excellence in health sciences education

Concern for society

- Fostering a spirit of scholarly inquiry in all of our activities and supporting exemplary health sciences research in selected areas

Specific products/ services offered

Distinctive competence

- Strengthening our relationships with universities, colleges, other hospitals, agencies, and the community we serve

Unique identity

Concern for society

- Demonstrating social responsibility and the just use of our resources.

Concern for owners

The commitment of our staff, physicians, volunteers, students, community partners, and friends to our mission permits us to maintain a *quality of presence* and *tradition of caring* that are hallmarks of Sunnyvale Metropolitan Hospital.

Unique identity

SIX

Communication

Bringing Your Hospital's Mission to the Masses

COMMUNICATION in its most general sense is the passing of a message from a sender to a receiver. The way in which Communication "success" is achieved, however, is through a *process.* Consequently, it is generally acknowledged that the better the process of communicating the mission—as measured in terms of its effect on human behavior—*the more successful it will be in putting your hospital that much closer to becoming 'mission-driven'.*

Not surprisingly, studies of the relationship between 'mission dissemination' and performance are rare. Nevertheless there is growing evidence that a strong correlation exists between employees' knowledge of their organization's mission and their commitment to it.

PART 1

Communication and Mission

To comprehend the significant role that Communication plays in facilitating the creation of the mission-driven hospital, this chapter examines two specific areas in which Communication interacts with a hospital's mission:

- The effectiveness with which the mission statement was communicated throughout the hospital and to its various stakeholders; and
- The Communication styles and methods used to disseminate the mission to the organization—as well as, again, their effectiveness

The viewpoint taken is that it is the actual dissemination of a hospital's mission statement—its Communication to and throughout the organization—that ultimately determines whether it is seen as a viable, energizing template for action or a moribund, uninspiring motherhood platitude.

Many practical suggestions are offered to show you how you can improve the degree to which your hospital's mission is both accepted and deployed through appropriate and effective Communication.

PART 2

The Mission-Implementation Process: Sending the Message

As discussed in Chapter 4 (Creation), the *mission development process* involves much participation and consultations among hospital stakeholders "arranged" in a style which, if it is to be effective, is open, flexible and creative. But what happens once "the powers that be" declare the development process complete, the hospital mission statement agreed to and written in final form? Indeed, an interesting mistake senior managers often make is to assume that when everyone is involved in a mission's creation, there is little need for continuing communication about it.

There is an important fact about any written document or new policy: *its impact is negligible unless it is read, understood and "absorbed."* Accordingly, a mission statement is useless unless it is well Communicated to all hospital stakeholders and internalized by them. A hospital's leadership, therefore, must consider what needs to happen *after* the mission statement is written—to whom, and in what way, is the mission communicated and communicated effectively.

In terms of '*mission communication frequency*,' I discovered that the CEO, senior managers, the board of directors, middle managers, non-managers and patients-clients were the dominant stakeholders to whom 95% of the hospitals tried to Communicate their mission statement. The hospitals also publicized their mission statements to shareholders/funders, consultants and suppliers at least 50% of the time. Thus, all hospital stakeholders are at least told about the 'finalized' mission statement in some way.

I also found that the highest level of reported '*effectiveness in Communicating the mission*' occurred with the internal stakeholder groups (including the board of directors). For the other stakeholder groups, most hospitals felt that their missions were Communicated at least "somewhat" or "moderately" effectively. Very few hospital managers believed that their hospital mission statements were Communicated ineffectively—which, in itself, says a lot!

Does The Effectiveness Of Communication Matter?

Upon reflection, it is not so surprising that hospital managers put more effort into Communicating—and Communicating effectively—their hospital's mission to some stakeholder groups than to others. After all, *internal stakeholders* are considered to be the most important audience to enlist in implementing a hospital's mission statement.

However, upon further analysis, I also found that the more the hospitals worked at effectively Communicating their mission to *almost all* stakeholder groups, the greater the ratings for *almost all* the outcome performance measures. Thus, there appears to be a clear performance benefit for those hospital managers who commit to investing the necessary effort to Communicate *effectively and broadly* their hospital's mission so that it is *known, understood and remembered by both internal and key external constituents.*

Interestingly, putting more emphasis on Communicating effectively to both patients-clients and shareholders/funders—two of the less attended to stakeholder groups—offered some of the strongest contributions to becoming mission-driven. One reason for this may be the fact that once patients are aware of the mission, they bring it to the attention of employees and put pressure on them to live up to its message ("Is THAT what you call "quality sensitive care", Doctor??") And once employees know that *"others know"*, they may put even more pressure on themselves to pay attention to delivering the messages contained in the mission. This latter observation therefore suggests that hospital administrators would benefit greatly by being more diligent in Communicating their mission to their patient-clients and shareholders/funders than they currently are—or at least as diligent as they are with their internal stakeholders.

Multi-Media Is The Message!

Communicating a hospital's mission, however, is not just a matter of "to whom" but also a matter of "how" the message is delivered. After all, not all *methods of message delivery* are equally effective for all people, nor are they equally effective under all circumstances. Visual messages (written memos, signs, posters, etc.) can be effective in that they can be read once and read again, assuming they are read in the first place. Oral messages can be effective if the speaker is vibrant and the listener happens to be an "aural" learner rather than a "visual" one. Trying to undertake effective Communication of an important message, like a hospital's mission, thus often means that you need to invoke multiple ways to get that message across.

Of the eight mission-dissemination methods used by hospital administrators (i.e., newsletters, advertisements, posters/plaques, word of mouth explanations of the mission (by superiors to subordinates), annual reports, seminars/workshops, company information kits, and employee manuals) the most frequently used methods were:

- The annual report
- Posters/plaques
- Employee manuals

Advertisements were the least frequently used method.

Despite these differences in usage, however, the hospital managers were quite consistent in their evaluation of how successful they considered each method to be in terms of communicating the mission. The respondents claimed that each method was only 'somewhat' to 'moderately successful'. Interestingly, among the Communication methods that received the highest scores as "extremely successful" were "word of mouth explanations of the mission (by superiors to subordinates). posters/plaques (the third most frequently used method), and advertisements (the least frequently used method!).

Does the Medium Matter?

Given these patterns of use, the obvious question now is: *do the methods of communicating the mission have anything to do with hospital performance and becoming mission-driven?* My subsequent analysis determined that 'word of mouth' and 'posters/plaques' had the most robust relationships with performance while the 'annual report' had absolutely none. Accordingly, hospital managers would appear to be well-served by focusing on the two 'top tier' communication methods since they individually seem to have the most far reaching impact on all the factors which contribute to making a hospital mission-driven. Concurrently, since a hospital's mission publication in the annual report appeared to have no impact on outcomes, hospitals may want to minimize their reliance on this outlet.

However, my most interesting observation on the topic of Communication was that when *all* Communication methods were considered together, they produced the highest impact on the various performance outcomes. One explanation for this is that by *relentlessly repeating* the mission message (and its interpretation), it generates the best understanding of a mission's content and promotes its "remembrance." As a learned professor once observed: It's not what we read that makes us educated; it's what we remember. A mission statement can only have a continuing impact in the life of an organization to the degree that organizational members can regularly recall it for guiding their daily resource allocation and decision making activities. Thus, it appears, as with broadly enlisting stakeholder groups' participation, that *mission Communication is more effective when multiple methods are used and used frequently.*

This "multi-media" result also appears to make a lot of sense because *the greater emphasis a hospital places on disseminating its mission statement, the more various stakeholders will believe in and identify with it.* Unfortunately though, while using all Communication methods would appear to be best, the cost of such an undertaking may be prohibitive. Nevertheless, the message above is that hospital management should use as many Communication methods *as possible* to demonstrate to stakeholders that the mission is being taken seriously.

Quality: The Key To Good Communication

I also uncovered another interesting message for those devising a hospital mission exercise: *as noted in Chapter 5, the quality of expression of a hospital mission's Content affects performance outcomes significantly.* This is not surprising given that we expect missions to inspire and energize stakeholders; effective expression should facilitate these outcomes. This is not to say that hospital mission statements need to be literary masterpieces, but they should encapsulate the mission's message (the Content) clearly, succinctly and in language appropriate to the mission's audience.

Significantly, I have determined that the need for quality of expression is not limited only to writing a hospital's mission statement. Indeed, to ensure success for both the process of development and dissemination of the mission, all of a hospital's mission related messages—as represented in the nine communication methods—must be properly expressed. After all, a hospital's success in becoming mission-driven ultimately equates with its organization members' understanding and internalizing of the mission. As one hospital manager volunteered on his returned survey: "*A beautifully crafted mission statement that is poorly developed and poorly sold is a sterile document.*" It is therefore imperative that the mission be written *and* Communicated (disseminated) *well*. If it is not, the performance outcomes (as contemplated here for making a hospital mission-driven) will be low and there will be little interest in the mission.

PART 3

Some Concluding Thoughts

Effective communication means that a message has been properly sent, received, understood, and remembered. Indeed, for a mission statement to be a living instrument within any hospital, it is important for each and every internal stakeholder to be able to recall, fairly accurately, its contents. When this occurs, they will be able to refer to it and to make the mission part of their day-to-day decision making processes.

Accordingly, I have argued in this chapter that appropriate mission dissemination processes have a powerful relationship with a hospital's performance outcomes and success with the mission. Hopefully, through this research, I have shown that hospital managers need to consider seriously the impact of the following issues when they develop and Communicate their hospital's mission statement:

- The stakeholders to whom the mission should be Communicated
- The need for Communication effectiveness;
- The Communication methods used to disseminate the mission statement; and
- The quality with which a Communication method is deployed.

To the extent that hospital managers genuinely and thoughtfully consider these items and handle them in a high-quality manner, their hospitals will be well on the way to both creating mission statements that matter and driving better organizational and individual performance. But that can't happen until the principles and research from the next chapter are embraced by hospital administrators, sections devoted to my fourth and fifth "C's": Coordination and Control, the final components required to make a hospital's mission statement a reality.

A MINI "MISSION COMMUNICATION" CASE EXAMPLE

Background

In 2010, the senior leadership of Reeves Memorial Hospital (RMH) determined that the organization's founding (and largely unwritten) mission 'was no longer being taken seriously enough or practiced sufficiently'. Accordingly, the hospital's executive team embarked on a journey to capture, write down and inculcate throughout the organization the purpose and values upon which the hospital was originally founded. Those still with the hospital today recall that developing the initial mission statement and making it real for all of their stakeholders was considered to be a one of the highlights of their working career.

Communicating the Mission

RMH uses numerous methods to Communicate its mission. For instance, once RMH formalized its mission, senior managers proceeded to concurrently clarify and give more details about the mission through two related documents. They are:

- The RMH Role Statement
- The RMH Management & Organizational Philosophy

Each of these documents expands on the mission and provides *interpretive guides* to the way in which the RMH mission should *direct day-to-day tasks* throughout the organization as well as strategic planning and resource allocation. Taken together, they comprise a powerful driving force for the organization.

A biennial review of the RMH mission also offers an in-depth opportunity for sending and receiving questions and concerns about the mission. The review process reinforces and re-affirms organizational 'intentions and expectations' and aids stakeholders' understanding of the mission—especially the internal constituencies. Senior managers, in particular, are charged with responsibility for responding to staff questions and comments about it, thereby deepening comprehension throughout the organization of the messages contained in the mission.

Additionally, RMH utilizes the standard vehicles (e.g., posters and plaques, internal documents and newsletters) to routinely Communicate its mission—as well as several that are unique to the organization. For instance: a mission-awareness workshop is held annually as a way to renew and refresh understanding of the mission. In one workshop, each RMH department was asked to create a poster that displayed the way in which the mission values were evident in their lives. Staffers have also been asked to submit designs for a "button," or badge to promote mission throughout the organization. In another session, all employees were asked to submit short essays describing what RMH would "look like, sound like, feel like, smell like and taste like". Each of these activities represent excellent ways to encourage involvement and heighten awareness of the mission's potential impact on all individuals.

There is also a twice-a-year Lunch and Learn Clinic dedicated to making mission come alive in the workplace. During the clinic, employees from different areas of the hospital come together to witness the way in which other employees' put the mission into action. According to the CEO, "This program is a great way to Communicate the role of the mission in a special situation. The Lunch and Learn program truly keeps the mission alive in the organization. Employees are inspired by the mission-driven behaviors of their colleagues which they would not have known about due to the large scale of the organization." The clinic therefore serves as an ongoing reminder that mission at RMH is expected to be part of everyday operations not just a formal occasional acknowledgement of mere words.

To its credit, RMH displays the mission prominently throughout its facilities (e.g., in the boardroom, the lobby and individual offices). As well, the staff newsletter, the *Reever Review,* routinely includes articles on "Living the Mission" which concentrates on a specific value contained in the mission and describes how that value can be manifested in everyday activities at RMH. That particular value is also simultaneously featured/posted throughout RMH and each department is instructed to determine how it will promote and exemplify this value in their own department. The Reever Review also includes a regular feature called "Mission Alive", which showcases an employee who consistently exhibits the RMH mission and values. The honoree is nominated by his peers and managers and is recognized throughout the organization for his/her efforts.

Another unique Communication vehicle at RMH is the presence of a 'mission tent' at the annual RMH picnic. The tent showcases the RMH mission statement along with departmental displays on the way in which RMH and its various departments provide specific/unique contributions to and interpretations of the mission. Significantly, the mission tent doesn't just reinforce the message to its staff, it acquaints the visiting families and community members with the importance of RMH's mission and how seriously it is taken by RMH. Even extensive new construction and renovation at RMH could not stop this activity. When this occurred, the tent was temporarily replaced with small 'floor picnics' for the patients and invited guests.

Direct Communication about the RMH mission also takes place when new employees are hired and when new patients arrive. In both instances, RMH takes the opportunity to make the 'new hires' aware of what the organization stands for. For employees, this means that they understand clearly that the mission values are vital criteria in their performance appraisal and therefore should not be ignored. For patients and their families, it's an opportunity for RMH to explain its values and the successful services it is able to provide as a result of *living them everyday*—services that it believes to be its competitive advantage.

One of the outgrowths of RMH's mission Communication activities is that individual departments have begun to create their own mission statements. It is instructive that, at one time, the senior management at RMH frowned on this development because they were worried that departmental missions might dilute and detract from the main RMH mission and confuse various constituents/stakeholders. However, departmental missions continue to peacefully co-exist because their purpose is only to show the way in which a department intends to apply the 'mother mission' to its activities. Because each departmental mission is tightly linked to and seeks ONLY to expand the interpretation of the RMH mission, the initial fears of senior management were completely allayed.

Other innovative RMH mission Communication efforts include a periodic radio program on a local AM radio station called "Ask the Experts." On these programs, RMH staff and volunteers have talked and answered questions about RMH's programs and services for patients while publicizing its core mission values to a broad community. In addition, RMH has produced a "Tradition in Caring" brochure which includes the mission statement and descriptions of RMH's facilities and services. This brochure was also included in the season-ticket packages of a local major sports team as well as an edition of the city's newspaper and displayed in all RMH entrances.

As a special Board activity, each member is required at each meeting to do a short presentation on the way in which they believe RMH lives its mission. This requires homework and advance preparation. Given their success with this activity, the Board later recommended that a different member of staff be invited to each Board meeting and asked to reflect on the way in which he/she demonstrates the mission in his/her position. Employees are randomly selected from all over the organization and asked to participate. They are, however, free to decline the invitation. According to the CEO, this new effort is highly educational and proves beneficial both to staff and to the Board since it serves to increase their mutual understanding of the mission.

Thus, RMH uses a number of methods frequently to Communicate its mission and keep it vital for its stakeholders. The mission had a solid introduction to RMH's stakeholders and continues to be Communicated to them in a variety of methods that engages all types of stakeholders—managers, staff, and external parties. As a result, employees report that they recognize the mission's meaning and import and they try diligently to use it to guide their behavior every day.

SEVEN

Coordination and Control
The Essential Ingredients for Aligning your Hospital with the Mission

COORDINATION AND CONTROL are the final parts of the "5-C" Mission Model that the hospital survey examined in detail. But a 'reminder warning' is in order at this point: *a hospital can't even begin to deal with these final two C's until it has determined the appropriate wording (Content) of its mission—based on sound principles of development (Creation)—and devised and executed a broad process of high quality dissemination (Communication).* The necessary next *and final* step of a hospital becoming truly mission-driven is: **ensuring that all internal stakeholders, principally the front line employees, internalize, embrace and "live" the mission.**

But how does a hospital *ensure* that this happens?; that the meaning of its mission (and the messages embedded in it) is actually embraced? One very good starting point is to persuade (and perhaps even demand that) all employees commit the mission to memory and to then use all of the Communication tools discussed in Chapter 6 (but especially plaques, posters and on-going word of mouth dialogues and discussions) to keep the mission in the forefront of everyone's minds. This is what happens with the mission statement ('Credo') at Johnson and Johnson (Exhibit 2 in Chapter 2) and as a result, the words and phrases contained in it are routinely 'plucked out' to populate the everyday and ordinary course of conversation at the company. And naturally, it is the top executives at J&J who have taken the lead (and continuously lead by example) in maintaining this critical component of their culture as a mission-driven organization.

However, the most powerful way for driving a hospital's mission to the front-line and thereby making it an on-going part of everyday operations, is to integrate the mission tenets into every aspect of the hospital's policies and organizational systems. And this is precisely what Coordination and Control are specifically designed to do: *they force organizational alignment with the mission* which, in turn, finalizes the creation of the mission-driven hospital. Moreover, Coordination and Control together virtually guarantee that your hospital's mission document will *never again* be seen as a sterile, ineffective statement—the most common complaint regarding this important strategic document!! It will become the new bible, the new 'good news' from whence every employee will derive a sense of belonging, ownership and purpose! Don't believe me? Read on.

PART 1

Coordination and Control—Fitting the Meaning of Mission with Structure

At the end of the day, the tangible expression of any organization's mission only occurs through the behavior and actions of its members. It does not matter how good a mission sounds or how well it reads. It does not even matter if everyone knows, understands and remembers the mission if it is not somehow practiced in the day-to-day activities of an organization's members. For this to happen, the dual concepts of Coordination and Control provide a simple, yet important management wisdom: if an organization has certain mission *end-results* in mind—say, patient-client or employee satisfaction—then *ALL of its policies, procedures, structures and systems must somehow support, reflect, promote and facilitate these mission goals.* Or, put another way, in order for any mission to be successfully implemented through the behaviors and actions of every staff person, all organizational systems must be **aligned** with it.

To the extent that this alignment does not exist, there will be a noticeable disconnect between what patients-clients thought they could expect of their healthcare organization (based on the mission statement prominently displayed in the lobby and examining rooms) and what hospital employees actually delivered. And the result will be stakeholder confusion. Patients will be confused and upset that they are not receiving the kind of care Communicated in the written mission statement—and wonder why not. Moreover, employees will be confused and frustrated with upset patients who seem to be demanding a level of care that no one else in the hospital appears to be concerned about. *"After all, isn't the mission statement just a slogan or advertising technique. No one here really takes it very seriously."* wrote one respondent CEO on his returned survey.

To create the necessary alignment, the usual starting point for management is to help employees *in every job* translate the mission's words and phrases into specific behaviors and actions which, for their particular job/position, reflect the priorities imbedded in the mission. For example, the mission phrase of "display a caring attitude" might be interpreted by the nursing team to mean "address all patients by their names in conversations with them". For the housekeeping staff, the same mission phrase might be translated to mean "ask the guest if there is anything else you can do for them before you leave the room—then try to fulfill their request, or find someone who can". For the accounting department, it might mean "develop decision criteria which encourages investments in caring-related activities".

Simply saying that "everything we do supports the mission" is either self-delusional (to simply make oneself feel good about the mission) or an attempt to avoid the hard work associated with defining "mission-specific" behaviors.

Once specified, though, such behaviors and actions still might not happen automatically. To ensure that they actually occur and often, requires additional alignment initiatives on the part of senior management—particularly in the way that a hospital's organizational systems are set-up to encourage, induce, and reinforce the behaviors/activities desired. For instance, many employees are often afraid of the behavioral challenges posed by a new mission because they feel that they will not know how to do (or be too embarrassed to do) the new tasks (e.g. "at all times, speak to the patient with a calmly sweet and reassuring voice"). Consequently, training and coaching programs may have to be developed and launched to ensure that employees have the necessary skills, attitudes and competencies required to carry out the new mission-inspired tasks. Similarly, when hiring new staff, hospital administrators should try using their mission statements as part of the interview, asking interviewees what they think the words in the mission statement mean and how they personally might make a contribution to the achievement of the mission.

Yet, despite these efforts, there are still two other major organizational processes that may need to be _Coordinated and Controlled_ with the mission if the desired behaviors are to be practiced on a regular basis. These are the organization's information and reward systems. Senior hospital administrators therefore must be prepared to take the necessary steps to measure and report on the degree to which any newly specified mission-related actions and behaviors are performed according to standard. In addition, a system of incentives (and disincentives) needs to be created to both encourage and coax the required mission-associated actions and to acknowledge/reward the behavioral performance of those whose commitment to living the mission on a daily basis is truly outstanding.

Thus, it is only though the _C_oordination and _C_ontrol of task specification, training, hiring criteria, performance measurement and incentives that an organizational context is formed in which the actions of all organizational members can be aligned with the mission. Indeed, my previous research concerning the effects of _C_oordination and _C_ontrol on mission in for-profit firms found that the degree of alignment between an organization's mission and its organizational practices produced some of the most powerful and positive relationships with various measures of performance. Accordingly, I wanted to see if the same held true in the case of not-for-profit hospitals.

PART 2

Coordination and Control in the Survey

Three questions were developed to examine the last two components of the 5-C Model in this study:

- To what extent do hospitals Coordinate and Control their organizational arrangements (i.e., formal structure, systems and processes) with their mission, *post development*?
- Does the degree of Coordination and Control of a hospital's organizational arrangements with its mission have any impact on performance and becoming mission-driven?
- Are there some specific organizational components whose Coordination and Control with a hospital's mission statement is more important than others?

To measure those organizational systems used by a hospital for Coordinating its activities in accordance with its mission, I assessed the:

- Organizational structure/design (the configurations, differentiation and integration of jobs)
- Job descriptions/job design
- Strategic-planning system (i.e., the process to set long-term goals and distinctive practices)
- Operating-planning system (i.e., the process to set short-term tactical plans)
- Budgeting system (i.e., the financial expression of the plans)
- General business objectives and targets
- Training/organizational development

To measure those organizational systems used by a hospital to Control its activities in accordance with the mission, I evaluated the:

- Recruitment system
- Employee performance-evaluation criteria
- Types of rewards

- Promotion system
- Leadership style (for demonstrating the mission through personal actions and behaviors)
- Management information (and 'performance measurement reporting') systems

Survey participants were asked to evaluate the *strength* with which each of these organizational components was aligned with their hospital's mission statement. They were also asked to rate their *degree of satisfaction* with the way in which each organizational component was selected, set up and managed. Finally, the performance measures referred to in previous chapters were used to assess the contribution of Coordination and Control with becoming a *mission-driven hospital*.

Do Hospitals Coordinate & Control their Organizational Systems to Fit their Mission?

Quite surprisingly, I found that very few of the hospitals in this study aggressively aligned their organizational systems with their mission statements! Rather, most hospital managers indicated that their hospital's mission was only moderately Coordinated and Controlled by their organizational arrangements. Nevertheless, some organizational components were more likely to be aligned with a hospital's mission than others. Interestingly, the most organizationally aligned components were those dealing with Coordination i.e. organizational structure, the strategic planning system, organizational objectives and targets, and the operating planning and budgeting systems. With the exception of "leadership styles" (which are used to exemplify the mission), none of the organizational arrangements associated with 'mission Control' appeared to be highly aligned.

An important finding, however, was discovered when the hospital managers' stated 'satisfaction with each organizational component' was compared with the degree to which each component was aligned with the mission. It was found that the more **any** of the elements of Coordination and Control are aligned with a hospital's mission, the more likely it is that managers will express satisfaction with the way in which that organizational component is structured and managed (and vice versa).

It was also fascinating to observe that the organizational systems least aligned with a hospital's mission (i.e. employee performance evaluation, reward, recruitment and information reporting systems) produced some of the strongest correlations with the satisfaction that managers claimed they had regarding how these organizational components were set up. (Recall that these systems were exclusively related to the notion of mission Control.)

Coordination, Control and Performance

Another interesting and important finding was discovered when the relationship between the organizational systems used to Coordinate and Control a hospital's mission implementation *and* the hospital performance indicators was investigated. More specifically, I found that, in every case, **there was a significant and positive relationship between the degree (or strength) of mission-organizational alignment and the performance measures.**

Investing In 'Mission-Organizational Alignment'

These findings suggest some important considerations for hospital managers attempting to create a mission-driven organization. A notable one is that the managers do, in fact, appear to align some of their organizational components with their mission statements more (conveniently) than others (but even then, not completely). In particular, they appear to favour those organizational systems which help Coordinate their mission's *dissemination and adoption* throughout the hospital over those systems used to Control its *implementation and restrain deviation from it*. Why would this be so?

The answer is simply that the task of aligning organizational components associated with 'mission Coordination' is easier than for 'mission Control'. For example: aligning the Coordination variable of 'organizational objectives' is, for most hospital managers, a relatively straight-forward and problem-free exercise with which most are familiar and comfortable. Also recall, as noted in the discussion of mission Content, that organizational objectives were considered for potential inclusion in the mission statement itself, but because of their nature (i.e., their specificity and temporal connection) they were found to be more appropriately "located elsewhere". Consequently, a parallel development of objectives with mission, thus aligning them together, is a reasonable occurrence.

In contrast, the organizational issues associated with aligning a mission Control mechanism such as a hospital's reward system— or its information system—will be much more challenging. This is because most hospital reward systems are often embedded in collective agreements for unionized employees. As such, they generally require wide agreement and negotiation to break through the inevitable political resistance that usually accompanies proposed changes. Similarly, changing a hospital's management information system to bring about (more or better) alignment is typically a time-consuming, complex and expensive undertaking. Therefore, some attempts to create the necessary Coordination and Control that comes with strong organizational alignment (and which signifies being mission-driven) are harder to do than others. Hopefully, this research has shown where, at least, the 'low hanging organizational fruit' now exists and for which organizational components hospital administrators should plan more time to create the alignment required.

The Satisfaction Factor and Alignment

Earlier it was noted that satisfaction with a hospital's existing organizational arrangements is associated positively with both the degree to which they help Coordinate the impregnation of the mission throughout the hospital and Control for employees' continuing commitment to it. This finding, however, can be interpreted in two intriguing ways:

One interpretation is that the more organizational systems are used to Coordinate and Control a hospital's mission, the more likely it is that managers will express satisfaction with the way in which those arrangements are structured and managed. In other words, high mission-organizational alignment begets satisfaction and agreement with organizational choices since now internal stakeholders can "properly value" and "see the logic in" the organizational decisions made. Or, put yet another way, high mission-organizational alignment validates both a hospital's mission and its organizational choices.

After all, most normal employees prefer to work in environments in which decisions about organizational arrangements make sense to them. They dislike work environments which are dysfunctional (i.e., hospitals at which the current organizational arrangements appear to be haphazard, random or spurious). Thus, to the extent that a hospital's organizational arrangements support and reflect the current mission (which they know and accept as valid), hospital employees derive comfort and satisfaction from it. When such alignment is absent, however, there is often confusion and anger with complaints resulting about the organizational choices made—choices that appear to be a "misfit."

But a second interpretation of the organizational satisfaction/ alignment result could also be this: those managers who are satisfied with their hospital's organizational arrangements (whatever they may be) will 'perceive' high degrees of alignment with the mission while *those who are not satisfied will invoke the argument of poor alignment as a way of expressing their displeasure.*

Although I really do believe that the first interpretation is the correct one (i.e., that high mission/organizational alignment creates high satisfaction), the causality of the association is not unequivocal. And so I will have to leave it to further research to ultimately determine which explanation carries the day.

PART 3

Mission Coordination and Control—The Performance Boost

As was shown in the chapters dealing with mission Creation, Content and Communication, taking the appropriate care to Coordinate and Control a hospital's organizational arrangements with its mission can have a profound impact on a hospital's performance. Indeed, the findings from this study offer *overwhelming support* for the importance of aligning virtually every organizational dimension with a hospital's mission. In every instance, **a hospital whose organizational**

arrangements were highly aligned with its mission was observed
to have a powerfully positive association with almost all of the outcome performance measures. Most importantly, in every instance,
the greater the mission-organizational alignment was, **the higher was
the reported satisfaction with the hospital's** *financial performance!*

Given these significant performance effects for mission-organizational alignment, it is somewhat surprising that managers in my
survey did not generally try to exercise—more aggressively—greater
Coordination and Control over their hospital's mission through more
tightly aligned organizational systems and processes.

One way to explain this dynamic is that the hospital managers
in this survey were simply not aware of the growing strategy literature that supports strong connections between strategy and a hospital's organizational arrangements. (My research on hospital mission
statements reported here thus represents an extension of this line of
thinking.) And to the extent that hospital managers were unfamiliar
with these ideas, they would also be ignorant of the various performance benefits accruing to those hospitals that seek and achieve
strong mission-organizational alignment.

That said, there could still be two other reasons for the observed
lack of whole-hearted commitment to the notion of mission-organizational alignment. The first is that the existing political climate
in the respondents' hospitals makes such efforts at changes in the
established organizational procedures extremely difficult. Another
related reason (discussed earlier) most likely arises from the relative
difficulty in implementing the necessary Coordination and Control
mechanisms with the mission. Nevertheless, based on the performance results discussed above, **hospital administrators are well
advised to find ways to increase the connections between their
missions and all their organizational arrangements** (i.e., the mechanisms for achieving organizational Coordination and Control with
the mission) since there appear to be strong benefits to those hospitals that are able to do so.

Moreover, if hospital managers want to improve on the way in
which their hospitals can become (more) 'mission-driven', they
might want to give special consideration to those organizational systems related to mission Control (which was observed to be more

weakly aligned with mission than the organizational mechanisms used for mission Coordination). I would not contend, however, that hospital managers should only try to align these Control aspects of their hospital with their mission—and, concomitantly, to downplay or ignore the others. Rather, as I have indicated above, high levels of *overall mission-organizational alignment* are capable of producing some of the strongest correlations with *overall hospital performance*. This fact alone underscores the synergistic effect that aligning each (and every) organizational component has with mission. *And it shows what it takes to become a truly mission-driven hospital!*

PART 4

A Final Word on Coordination and Control Alignment with Mission

As I wind up my commentary on the last of the 5-Cs, my findings suggest some important implications for hospital administrators relating to their efforts to become mission-driven. The first is that, notwithstanding the important and necessary contributions of Creation, Content and Communication to becoming a mission-driven hospital, it is Coordination and Control that define and cause activities to be produced and practiced among all organizational members. Accordingly, it is imperative that hospital managers not shy away from aligning their organizational components with their hospital mission just because of the difficulties associated with doing so. Any organizational change will always cause disruption and unease but the payoffs associated with Coordinating and Controlling the mission appear to be so dramatic that hospital managers should diligently commit to making any and every necessary change to create the strongest possible mission-organizational ties. This is the only way of encouraging and ensuring the highest possible overall performance benefits to their institutions. . . . something that only being mission-driven can produce.

The second major implication of my survey is the temporal one. Alignment of a hospital's organizational systems to its mission

requires change but change needs to be debated and eventual acceptance requires time. This may involve a demanding and comprehensive process. Accordingly, a simple 'quick and dirty' top-down
"fitting" of mission-organizational alignment may not be enough for
all aspects of the systems. Enough time must be allotted to integrate
a hospital's mission throughout the entire organization (and all of its
activities) if real success with a hospital's mission is to be achieved

Finally, as with the other parts of the **5-C Mission Model**,
Coordination and Control of mission do really matter—a lot! Over
the last decade, the need for hospitals to better Coordinate and
Control their organizational systems with their mission is now a
critical strategic imperative. Massive change has been taking place in
the healthcare systems of countries world-wide due to funding cuts
and increased pressure to find new efficiencies in operations. But at
the same time, it must always be remembered that *hospitals have a
social purpose/mission and not just an economic one.* This entails having a special kind of commitment to its non-economic stakeholders:
patients-clients, employees and the community at large.

The relationship which a hospital needs to create, maintain
and enhance with these 'other stakeholder's is what I found to be
important components in the Content of a great mission statement
(Chapter 4). Thus, enhancing strong organizational Coordination
and Control with the mission (which would not ignore these 'other
stakeholders') should help to achieve the traditional social healthcare mandate even as contemporary reengineering and reorganiza-
tions of hospitals occur to increase their 'efficiency'. In other words,
Coordination and Control of a hospital's organizational systems with
the mission can serve as a focal point to help facilitate a smooth tran-
sition for all stakeholders as a result of the dramatic—and sometimes
brutal—changes taking place around them. It is Coordination and
Control that provide the insurance that a hospital's mission will realize its fullest potential.

A MINI "COORDINATING & CONTROLLING THE MISSION" CASE EXAMPLE

Background

In 1990, the Baxter Health Sciences Corporation (BHS) was formed through a merger of two hospitals. The amalgamation included four site locations and was designed to create *efficiencies* and encourage centres of excellence in *targeted healthcare specialties:* a children's hospital, cancer treatment, cardiac cases, trauma and burns.

BHS employs more than 10,000 staff, among which are over 2,800 nurses and 1,000 medical doctors. It's annual operating budget exceeds $1.0 billion.

Bringing together the four facilities was no easy task since the organizational culture of each primarily independent hospital was unique. In fact, the melding of operations—such as management information systems—and bringing together staff, including unionized groups, under a single aegis is still evolving. A major BHS unification tool has been the development of its mission statement in 1991, with an accompanying vision and values statement. The hospital has since excelled in inculcating the mission into the everyday actions and behaviors of its entire staff by Coordinating and Controlling all organizational systems with the mission.

Coordinating and Controlling the Mission at BHS

From the time of the BHS mission's creation in 1991, the hospital's executives recognized the need to create a formal program dedicated to ensuring the mission's successful implementation. As a result, over the years, *a number of organizational initiatives have kept BHS's operations and activities aligned with its mission* and, in so doing, in the forefront of hospital stakeholders.

Mission Coordinator. In 1992, for example, a Director of Mission was hired to ensure that the mission statement would become and remain a 'living document that motivated hospital staff'. This was a senior management position which thereby signaled the true value and magnitude of mission to BHS on a on-going, daily basis. Also, with the exception of the CEO, the Director of Mission's job overarches all other organizational positions. Its incumbent there-fore serves not just as a critical Communication vehicle but also as an important mechanism to Coordinate and Control the *inclusion of mission in all high-level BHS administrative decisions.*

The Director of Mission stated that BHS is deeply committed to quality and especially committed to its employees because satisfied employees are more likely to embrace the mission and bring it alive. She said that, in the often routinized, deadeningly repetitive job environment of patient care, having satisfied employees is critically necessary, and especially more so when staffers are limited in the amount of time they can spend with individual patients because they have to treat so many." Accordingly, she helped develop a "Quality of Life" (QOL) survey that proved extremely beneficial in monitoring both patients' and employees' satisfaction at BHS. It routinely discovers pockets of concern requiring improvement.

Mission Focused Committees. In 1995, new government policies directed BHS to rationalize its health services. Accordingly, the CEO established a Mission Renewal Committee to recognize and accom-modate this new 'stakeholder reality'. However, he also appointed a 'facility dedicated' mission coordinator to assist his hospital staff (medical and voluntary) in remaining true to the BHS mission. At the same time, the Board of Directors established a Mission Effectiveness Committee to evaluate how well the mission was being applied and to ensure that future projects reflected the new mission's values. As a result, the Board obtained a direct line-of-sight on the hospital's ongoing efforts at maintaining and improving BHS's stakeholder relations.

BHS also formed a Quality Healthcare and Values Committee, which is charged with ensuring that the values embodied in the mission are reflected in monitoring hospital quality and setting policy. One of its chief activities is to gather feedback from all BHS programs on patient care and satisfaction, as well as processes that integrate BHS's mission with hospital operations. This committee thus serves 'double duty' by simultaneously Communicating the success of the BHS mission while acting as an organizational cata-lyst for integrating and aligning the mission with all aspects of hos-pital operations.

<u>Awards and Recognition.</u> Additionally, BHS has instituted a number of awards to increase behavioral <u>C</u>ontrol over the mission's execution. These awards are given annually to individual "missionaries" and groups who have demonstrated extraordinary efforts in aligning the BHS mission with their daily activities. The Commitment to Caring award (for an individual) and Working Together award (for groups) are just two examples. Another is the Jack Robinson Award, which honors the teacher and clinician who best exemplifies the values embedded in the mission. These are "grass roots awards" whereby employees must be nominated for them by their colleagues. Winners receive a framed plaque, and a $50 gift certificate. They are also recognized in the BHS newsletter and their pictures displayed in the hospital lobby. The numerous nominations of staff for these awards suggest the high degree to which the BHS mission is exemplified throughout the organization and that employees realize the importance of mission-value-laden behavior in enhancing patients' lives. Finally, BHS has both 'appreciation nights' for volunteers and 'length-of-service-award nights' for staff which routinely recognize and link their contributions to the success of the BHS mission.

Plans are also in the works to increase the frequency with which the hospital formally recognizes those employees who have exemplified the BHS mission in their lives and work. Rather than recognizing individuals only once a year, the hospital intends to establish 'monthly mission champions' who would be recognized through banners or plaques in the hospital. These individuals will also be the subject of a dedicated section in the bi-weekly newsletter. This will create the potential to recognize approximately 50 individuals annually.

<u>Strategic Planning.</u> Strategic planning is also another very important way in which the major activities and initiatives of the hospital are linked to achievement of the mission. At BHS, the strategic plan uses the hospital's mission as its starting point and then translates its key components into a set of coordinated goals, objectives, indicators, outcomes and benchmarks *that help evaluate whether BHS is on target in achieving its mission goals.*

For example, BHS's current strategic plan focuses on: academic excellence; the values of respect and caring; and the uniqueness of its providing healthcare to underprivileged inner-city residents and street dwellers. These strategic priorities derive specifically from the hospital's mission statement and BHS has, in large measure, both translated them into action plans and dedicated resources to them in order to ensure their fruition. In the words of one Vice-President at BHS: "The mission priorities are integrated into all of BHS's planning and resource-allocation decisions." Importantly, the strategic plan is also renewed periodically and the goals and directions reassessed— always, though, to be in line with the mission. Thus, at BHS, their mission is central to the strategic level and therefore guides high-level managerial decision-making.

Moreover, as part of the hospital's 'mission commitment' to inclusiveness in decision making, employees and volunteers have representation on board and executive committees thereby providing a crucial link between those with broad based knowledge of a mission-driven strategic plan (i.e. the board) and those responsible for its successful implementation (i.e. the staff—especially the front-line).

Human Resources Policies. Similarly, throughout the various revisions of its mission, BHS has worked diligently and demonstrably to manage and align its human resources policies and procedures with its mission. To formalize this alignment, BHS initiated in 2003 a Mission At Work Program (MAW). The MAW program identified four key mission values: service, respect, responsible stewardship and community responsiveness. These values formed the basis for a comprehensive HR system overhaul which included employee appraisals, job descriptions, hiring and interviews as well as orientation. While BHS had informally linked mission to these HR functions in the past, the MAW program brought the BHS mission front and centre to each of the following HR activities:

Job Postings: MAW developed a standard approach to job postings, naming the position, the department that houses the position and the reporting relationship of the position. Most importantly there is a new section, the Mission Impact Statement, which briefly describes how each particular job aligns with the BHS mission.

Job Interviews: Before MAW was adopted, BHS gave each interviewee a copy of the mission statement and asked whether the applicant believed he or she could live up to it. With the adoption of the MAW protocol, each of the mission values is broken down into three or four competencies and 73 potential interview questions are available for use with respect to these. During interviews, managers are expected to ask candidates selections of these questions to identify individuals who most align with BHS's mission.

There is also the 'Self-Reflection Tool' which outlines ways in which the hospital expects new employees to translate the mission into their life and work. As part of this tool, candidates complete a questionnaire that helps to self assess their potential to fulfill the mission as employees. In the document, it states explicitly that "we recruit, select and develop personnel who carry out our mission in a manner consistent with our values." At the actual interview, candidates are expected to show understanding and appreciation for the importance of BHS's mission to their position. Even prospective board members are asked to write an essay on "how they will contribute to the BHS mission" so that the CEO and other Board members can better understand the character and values of the individual under consideration. Ostensibly then, recruiting and selection at BHS are tightly aligned with its mission.

Interestingly, 'mission achievement' is also a major factor considered in exit interviews with employees. These interviews are generally used to try to improve working conditions at BHS but at them, individuals are asked specifically to evaluate whether and how well BHS carries out its mission.

Performance Appraisal (PA): Prior to MAW, BHS asked employees only one question about their commitment to the hospital's mission during their performance appraisal: "Do you live the BHS mission?" The MAW Program, however, introduced a three-part evaluation:

- Definition of the mission values and competencies related to the position and the mission related behaviors required to be evaluated in the appraisal
- Performance requirements specific to the employee's department
- A performance-development plan measuring how well the employee met past goals and giving him or her the

opportunity to set future goals—especially those related to supporting the achievement of the mission

Through this process, all performance appraisals are directly linked to the mission. Qualitative measures and anecdotal accounts are used to measure 'mission fulfillment' as part of every employee's evaluation. For managers in particular, BHS's mission values are expected to drive their policies, standards and day-to-day decision-making. As with the CEO, managers at BHS are expected to be exemplars of the mission and one of their key result areas is 'mission integration'—the first of nine prime accountability measures. But, front-line staffers are expected to display mission behaviors as well in order to receive incentives and to continue employment. Even at the Board level, the annual self-evaluation of board members includes "Living the Mission" as a key measure.

Employee Orientation: This is an area in which BHS had already developed a mission-driven program prior to MAW's inception. Specifically, in 2002, as part of its 'I Make a Difference Campaign', the hospital prepared 'Living the Mission at BHS', a booklet given to all new hires that describes the mission and the hospital's commitment to it. As well, it outlines various standards of everyday behavior, including such routine activities as phone etiquette, that reflect the mission in action.

Employee Discipline: The BHS mission must be invoked as the justification for any employee disciplinary action- including giving even a reprimand but especially in the case of an employ termination.

Training and education: One of the ways that an organization tries to enhance its employees' experience and commitment is by offering them opportunities to expand their knowledge through education. Indeed, as BHS's mission states, it will "create an effective environment for learners and provide on-going educational opportunities for staff to enhance their knowledge and skills." Since healthcare is a competency-based industry, up-to-date knowledge is critical to providing effective and efficient patient care. BHS has worked to open more educational opportunities for staff by allocating resources directly for paid educational and training days. Applicants for training, however, must state how it will help them contribute to the BHS mission. And for in-house courses, instructors are required to open with a discussion on how the training reflects and reinforces the values and apsirations contained in the BMH mission.

Doing it right! Recently, BHS received a commendation for its quality care and service to the community. Moreover, it has success-fully undergone accreditation every three years and has been a four-time finalist for a major national healthcare award, twice winning for 'service to patients' and once winning the 'overall' award. The CEO and other senior managers believe this continued recognition of BHS's excellence to be tied directly to their dedication to living their mission "day in and day out, 24/7".

In conclusion, the use of numerous organizational arrangements to Coordinate and Control the implementation of BHS's mission is a study in relentless, near obsessive, continuous improvement. Since its first inception in 1991, the application of BHS's mission has grown and improved in all areas of its operations. And overall, it cannot be denied that BHS works very hard at trying to engage staff and imbue them with the mission-driven values of the organization.

EIGHT

Who Does It Better?
Faith-based vs. Secular Hospitals and Mission

AT THE BEGINNING OF THIS BOOK, I noted that the concept of mission and missionary zeal had a pre-eminent place in faith-based venues. Religions, by their very nature, include a belief system which involves *expected behaviors* in its adherents—behaviors typically based on caring and respect for others (albeit at times exclusive and discriminatory). Where religion has established itself in social institutions, such as education or healthcare, belief systems generally manifest themselves and direct the actions of the organization.

In the not-for-profit healthcare sector in Canada, faith-based hospitals are part of the landscape so I made a point of including them in my survey. I also thought it was important to try to determine *whether the underlying nature of the hospital*, whether it is secular or faith-based, *affects the way in which a hospital's mission is developed and implemented.* Thus, if faith-based hospitals actually "do" mission better than secular healthcare institutions, then perhaps something can be learned from their efforts.

Through my research, I came to realize that though secular hospitals do indeed differ philosophically from faith-based ones, *nowhere has any attempt been made to examine what makes the two operationally distinct.* Thus, I wanted to explore—and devote a chapter to—an examination of whether, in fact, faith-based hospitals differ from their secular counterparts with respect to the **5-C Mission Model** (**C**reation, **C**ontent, **C**ommunication, **C**oordination and **C**ontrol). Moreover, I wanted to assess especially whether there were any differences between the two types of hospitals with regard to their performance and, when all is said and done, the degree to which they are *mission-driven*.

So, do the 45 faith-based hospitals included in this study do a better job of developing and implementing their mission statements than the 95 secular ones? Let's find out.

PART 1

Mission and Hospital Performance

The discussion presented in previous Chapters *concerning the entire sample* should have, by now, emphasized the point that not any mission statement (or set of mission practices) will do; that mission statements which have been developed and disseminated in certain ways—and which contain certain types of information—appear to be associated with superior performance. Or, put another way, when certain mission practices occur, their *mission performance impact* is high i.e. mission is a greater energy source, a better guide to decision making, influences personal behavior more and results in greater satisfaction with financial performance.

The question that now remains, however, is whether the performance impact of an organization's mission practices is the same or different between faith-based and secular hospitals? Knowing the answer would offer some powerful evidence regarding the role and usefulness that mission statements play in each type of organization's success. It would also help in identifying those mission statement practices that may be associated or linked with any observed performance differences.

My investigation discovered that *faith-based hospitals (relative to the seculars) seemed to fare significantly better concerning the achievement of their mission*; that mission was, for them, a significantly greater source of energy; that they experienced significantly higher levels of employee commitment to the mission; and that their mission seemed to have a significantly greater degree of influence over the behavior of their organizational members.

Implications Stemming from the Performance Differences

Over the past 20 years, mission statements have received a lot of attention in both academic publications and the popular press. While most of the writing suggests that these documents are needed and necessary, there have been little empirical findings to support their use. Indeed, because of the scant evidence showing their performance impact, there has been a growing tendency (particularly within public sector organizations) to view mission statements as a necessary evil—something required for accreditation, but not much else.

The results from my analysis of the performance differences between secular and faith-based hospitals show that there are varying performance effects within different organizations and that, insofar as faith-based hospitals are concerned, the consequence for selected performance outcomes is much more positive and pronounced. Faith-based institutions appear especially to excel in terms of garnering significantly higher levels of emotional conviction behind their missions (which, of course, raises the question as to why the seculars either do not—or, cannot—do this too). Thus, in faith-based hospitals, mission statements seem to be powerful medicine.

Yet, interestingly, both types of hospitals also appear to share some of the same weaknesses. For instance, I found that there were two areas where the hospital performance measurement scores were relatively low and where there were no significant differences between faith-based and secular hospitals concerning them i.e. the mission being explicitly used as a guide to making decisions; and satisfaction with financial performance.

As pointed out earlier, one of the main values of a mission statement lies in its ability to provide a basis for daily decision making and allocating scarce resources in a more focused manner. My research now shows that this is one performance area where both faith-based and secular hospitals could benefit from greater concentration and emphasis.

Mission statements have also been shown to have some influence on financial performance. However, for our faith-based hospitals, satisfaction with financial performance was rated the lowest area of accomplishment. And even though this variable ranked first among the seculars in terms of their accomplishments, the overall performance score was still comparatively low.

Considering the tremendous changes and pressures being placed on all healthcare institutions for fiscal responsibility and restraint, how do we account for these results? Why are the reported financial satisfaction measures so low? And how do we explain the pattern obtained concerning the performance emphasis and differences between faith-based and secular institutions? I believe the answers to these questions lie in our discussion of the remaining findings.

PART 2

Creation

The Drivers of Mission

In my examination of the *mission drivers (rationales)* that lead faith-based and secular hospitals to create their mission statements, I found that only three were used to a statistically higher degree and all occurred in the faith-based hospitals:

- Promoting shared values;
- Creating behavior standards; and
- Motivating and inspiring employees

The remaining seven drivers showed no significant differences between hospital types.

This finding supports the conclusions reached in Chapter 4 about hospitals' choice of mission rationales: hospital managers have distinct preferences for certain mission drivers over others. Interestingly, the *ranking* of the mission rationales was essentially the same for both faith-based and secular hospitals. However, the three drivers used more frequently by the faith-based institutions seem particularly telling. Let me explain.

Given the strong value systems that underpin faith-based hospitals, it is not unusual to see the factors of 'shared values', 'behavioral standards' and 'employee motivation' as very important for a mission exercise. Indeed, for these hospitals, their grounding in religion has perhaps given them a better appreciation of the way in which shared values and behavioral standards enhance performance. More specifically, creating shared values and behavioral standards is an integral aspect of developing and maintaining an organization's faith-based culture.

But it should be noted that faith-based institutions do not have a stronghold on the **values/performance** relationship. Management researchers have long argued that when employees share the values of their organization, they are more likely to feel an emotional bond to a mission statement that reflects those values. A number of studies have also found that employees of organizations which are founded and grow from a strong "values base" have a greater commitment to mission. Furthermore, when behavioral standards become firmly established, they act as a form of inner self-control, automatically eliciting specific actions and tasks from employees that are congruent with mission and, thereby, improving the organization's focus. Accordingly, a strong 'values-based' organization is inevitably more attractive to both customers and employees—and more dangerous to competitors—than their counterparts.

Mission Drivers And Performance

I believe my findings regarding the mission drivers discussed above help explain the performance results we discussed earlier. In particular, the significantly higher performance outcomes achieved by faith-based hospitals (in terms of 'achievement of the mission', 'mission as energy source', 'mission influence on member behavior' and 'commitment to the mission') seem to be associated, quite naturally, with the significantly higher ratings they attained for certain mission drivers i.e. mission developed 'to promote shared values', 'to create behavior standards' and 'to inspire organizational members'.

In a similar vein, faith-based and secular hospitals were each found to have considerably low performance scores (that were not significantly different from each other) pertaining to the outcome measure "mission as a decision making guide". This finding, however, can also be explained by reference to the fact that both types of hospitals had comparatively low, and non-significant, scores for the mission rationale of "guiding resource allocation decisions".

These results suggest therefore that hospital managers should be *both* cautious about *and* yet need to understand explicitly the reasons for which they wish to develop their mission statements in the first place. My evidence suggests that there is a reasonably strong connection between the motivations that spawn a mission and the end results. Indeed, these observations bear witness to the wisdom in the old proverb "as ye sew, so shall ye reap".

Secular hospitals should be especially concerned with these findings since they imply that, for the most part, there are no significantly strong factors influencing the creation of their mission—at least, in terms of the way it appears to occur in faith-based institutions. If secular hospitals approach the mission development process with ambivalence, or disdain, they run the risk of either alienating their critical internal stakeholders (whose support for implementing the mission is crucial) or producing a document which is meaningless and trivial. To do either will deprive a hospital of the spirit and energy which many regard as one of the hallmarks of any great organization—especially, a "mission-driven" one.

These results, however, also give another cause for concern: *that resource allocation is not seen sufficiently enough as a major mission driver by either type of hospital.* The way in which an organization allocates its (scarce) resources is one of the most important activities that it can undertake and one of the most tangible expressions of its strategy. My findings imply that somehow this message has not gotten through or is being ignored in both types of institutions.

Personal discussions with hundreds of CEOs over the years, however, causes me to conclude that most hospital administrators' experiences with mission statements is so jaundiced (as "do nothing, go nowhere" documents and exercises) that they simply give them short shrift in terms of their usefulness. There has been little empirical evidence showing the economic benefits of deploying mission statements as a decision making and risk management tool.

But, the tide may be changing. As argued in Chapter 4, the objectives of creating shared values and a common direction are two of the most difficult outcomes for an organization to achieve. By contrast, using the mission statement for resource allocation may be one of the easiest to accomplish, bringing with it numerous performance benefits, including satisfaction with financial results. This is not to say that hospital managers should abandon their pursuit of creating shared values among their organizational members—for indeed, such pursuits represent one of the classic, timeless and important roles that mission statements can play. It is also a role that, based on my findings, hospital managers already understand and accept.

Hospital administrators, however, may be overlooking an easy way of accomplishing these two higher order objectives simultaneously. By linking the resource-allocation process to mission, they can both focus their strategy and motivate their employees *at the same time*. Hospital administrators thus need to rethink their motivations for having a mission statement and consider how they might better incorporate their mission into the resource-allocation process.

The Mission Creation Process: Does Religion Help?

In comparing how faith-based and secular institutions responded regarding their mission-Creation processes, I looked at three distinct aspects:

- The involvement/participation by different stakeholder groups
- The influence of different stakeholders groups, and
- The style of the development process

In terms of the first item, "stakeholder involvement", I observed that there were significant differences between faith-based and secular hospitals in only two instances—middle managers and shareholders/funders—and in each one, faith-based institutions had the higher involvement score. For the other seven classes of stakeholders, there was no significant difference.

When the 'level of influence' that various stakeholder groups had on the mission-development process was examined, only the shareholder/funder group was found to have a significantly higher influence and again the influence was greater in faith-based hospitals than in secular ones.

These results are interesting given the fact that, as discussed in Chapter 4, higher levels of participation (both involvement and influence) make a stronger contribution to becoming mission-driven. Broad involvement and influence means that more stakeholder needs and concerns are taken into account, resulting in the creation of the "right" mission statement to generate a greater sense of ownership from all stakeholder groups.

What I found, however, was that there is little difference between faith-based and secular hospitals with respect to their mission-development processes. Both types of institutions rely heavily for mission development on their CEOs, upper managements and the Board of Directors (ranked 1, 2 and 3 respectively) and generally ignored input from their non-managers (front-line staff), patients and suppliers (ranked 6, 7 and 9 respectively). Influence exerted by the latter stakeholders was shown to be considerably low as well. As noted above, middle managers and shareholders/funders participated significantly more in mission development at faith-based hospitals but only shareholders/funders exerted more influence there than at secular institutions, a fact which we shall discuss more in this chapter regarding mission Content.

These 'stakeholder involvement and influence' findings therefore parallel those noted in Chapter 4 and help to explain not only why employees appear to be absent from the Content of most mission statements in this study, but also why such low satisfaction scores were reported concerning the mission-development process—regardless of the type of institution. It seems that both secular and faith-based hospitals view their lower level employees as second-class citizens when it comes to crafting mission statements. This could perhaps be one factor that helps explain the growing degree of labour and union unrest that exists in healthcare today. This attitude, though, is counterproductive in light of the enormous performance advantages which appear to be associated with high stakeholder involvement. Consequently, I would counsel hospital managers everywhere to find ways to increase both the participation and the influence of all their stakeholders when they formulate or re-evaluate their missions—and ideally to a level equal to that of the CEO and senior managers.

While participation and influence are important and have an impact on 'satisfaction with the mission process', there is also another possible reason why hospital managers expressed unhappiness with their mission process. One that relates to the "style" with which it was conducted. I found that there were no significant differences in style between faith-based and secular hospitals.

In Chapter 4, I noted that the preferred mission process (i.e., one that conferred high satisfaction levels for mission Content and process) was one that was flexible, simple and creative and was produced from the "bottom up," rather than by autocratic, CEO or senior-management fiat. My observation in both faith-based and secular hospitals, however, indicates that the style of process reported by the majority of survey respondents did not embrace these dictums, certainly not in any wholehearted way. Instead, the mission processes deployed in the sample were often just 'middle-of-the-road' in their application. This, in turn, implies that they were more rigid, more complex or just plain more ordinary than they should have been. Accordingly, these observations help to explain the widespread lack of satisfaction with the mission development process.

It was also interesting to observe that for the sample of faith-based hospitals, they appeared to use cross-functional or cross-departmental teams to develop their missions to a significantly greater extent than the seculars. One reason for this may be that the managers in faith-based hospitals are more knowledgeable about the advantages of teams in managing a business process. Indeed, previous research has continued to reinforce the point that the use of teams is an important aspect of any mission development exercise. This is because teams help to take into account 'diversity of opinion' and thereby help create a mission statement that more accurately reflects the needs of the organization.

But rather than simply being 'more knowledgeable' than their secular counterparts, faith-based hospitals may also be using teams as a normal outgrowth of their values systems, which typically places a high value on "inclusiveness." The process of creating a mission is therefore an opportunity to practice that belief. And so, teams are used significantly more often.

Yet, there could also be a cynical and darker explanation for their greater use of teams: Administrators in faith-based hospitals may believe that, by using teams, their obligation to carry out the mandate of inclusiveness ends—a possibility that may also explain why few lower-level employees were either involved in the mission process or influenced it. By using teams, these hospital administrators can cleverly argue to their Boards that they do not need to seek broader participation than the cross-functional team itself and hence can speed up the mission development process considerably.

Whether faith-based hospitals used teams for good or bad reasons, their significantly higher use did not appear to increase substantially their 'satisfaction with the mission process' in comparison to their secular peers. Thus, while the use of teams contributes positively to a mission's Creation, the process still appears to need broad participation and influence to be a satisfying exercise.

PART 3

Mission Content—The Stuff of Which Mission Dreams Are Made

In Chapter 5 it was noted that six mission Content items were among the most popular identified by hospital respondents i.e.,

- Statement of purpose
- Statement of values/beliefs
- One clear compelling goal
- Specification of patients-clients served
- Specification of services/products offered
- Concern for satisfying patients

As a result, I suggested that the "choices" made by these administrators showed they had distinct preferences for the Content of their mission statements. For this chapter, I partitioned the frequency of mission Content items according to their faith-based or secular sources. Interestingly, the most frequent items for both types of institutions were essentially the same and similar to the overall samples reported in Chapter 5. Moreover, the rankings of the Content items were relatively the same for secular and faith-based hospitals, suggesting that both have the same tastes when it comes to creating a mission statement.

Looking more closely, however, I discovered that, despite this basic agreement, there were eight items that faith-based institutions specified to a statistically significant higher degree:

- Statement of values/beliefs
- Unique identity
- Concern for satisfying patients
- Distinctive competence/strength
- Specific behavior standards
- Desired competitive position
- Concern for satisfying shareholders'/owners'/funders' needs
- Competitive strategy

Looking back once again to Chapter 5, many of these Content items were the same ones that were found to have a significant correlation with the hospital performance indicators of interest to us in this Chapter.

Content and Creation—Articulating Mission Rationale

Of the eight Content items mentioned significantly more often by the faith-based hospitals, it is not surprising that many relate to *moral virtues* and how to conduct one's self. Indeed, the ubiquitous inclusion of these items by faith-based institutions represents the logical first step for articulating and expressing the *primary* 'mission rationales' from which their mission Content springs: to create shared values, to set behavior standards and to inspire employees.

Moreover, the Content items of 'unique identity', 'distinctive competence', 'competitive position' and 'competitive strategy' can be linked to faith-based hospitals' primary mission rationales as well. After all, if one is aiming to inspire organizational stakeholders (a major mission driver in faith-based hospitals), then articulating (i) a unique purpose that the organization is going to serve (e.g. *"To eliminate human misery and suffering among the poor, the disadvantaged and the unwanted in our city."*), (ii) a distinctive competence (e.g. *"We are renowned for our effective treatment of spinal cord as well as head and neck injuries"*) (iii) a desired competitive position (e.g. *"To be the best in the world at providing…"*, *"To be the most admired in our region for…; "To be ranked the number one hospital in our city!"*) and/or (iv) a competitive strategy (e.g. *"We will strive to provide our patients with outstanding service and give our employees a most rewarding professional working environment"*) can be extremely effective in terms of rousing human emotions and stirring the competitive soul.

But, there is also another reason to explain the significantly higher specification of these latter mission components in faith-based hospitals. Faith-based institutions (when compared with their secular sisters) may simply have a better understanding and appreciation of the way in which "unique identity", "distinctive competence", "desired competitive position" and "competitive strategy" enhance and contribute to the performance of their healthcare organizations. Because of this, they can be critical success factors for the survival of healthcare institutions—especially when confronting the current turbulent environment, which requires them to uniquely identify their competitive strengths, distinctive nature and abilities—something many faith-based hospital administrators who responded to our survey appeared to recognize.

It should be noted, however, that my observations and findings do not give faith-based hospitals the right to be complacent. In fact, 47% of the faith-based healthcare providers did not include desired competitive position in their mission statements while 59% made no mention of competitive strategy. Consequently, there is room for both secular *and* faith-based hospitals to reconsider the Content of their mission statements to ensure that the components they include are those that will help them realize their primary mission drivers.

In addition to the findings noted above, there were two other mission components that were found to receive considerably more attention and specification in the mission statements of faith-based hospitals. "Concern for satisfying patients", for example, was mentioned to a significantly higher degree than in the seculars—thereby indicating very high sensitivity on the part of faith-based hospitals to the needs and interests of this important stakeholder constituency. However, this finding did not come as too much of a surprise given the expressed values of most faith-based hospitals and their near *obsession* with serving the sick. (*"At our hospital, it is an honor to serve the sick."* is how one faith-based healthcare organization expresses it in their mission).

It was also not unusual to find a significantly higher expressed 'concern for shareholders/funders' (relative to the seculars) since most faith-based hospitals still have some ties with their founding faith-based orders and/or institutions that built them—often under arduous conditions. It was these 'founders' who invested the faith-based hospitals with specific values. The "original owners" today, though, are smaller in number and quite elderly. And their challenge now is to ensure a value-laden culture is sustained by staff and other stakeholders who usually have differing religious, cultural and economic beliefs. Thus, concern for these "shareholders" implies that faith-based hospitals want to ensure that the cultural values of the founders are not lost to the institution.

Despite the fact that 'concern for shareholders/funders' was mentioned significantly more frequent in the mission statements of faith-based hospitals (49%) than secular ones (26%), it is surprising that slightly more than half of the faith-based institutions did not include this item in their missions. One explanation for this observation may be that hospital administrators of faith-based institutions are simply unaware of its importance as a mission component and unknowledgeable of the performance benefits associated with its inclusion. If this were true, it would justify the recommendation that all faith-based hospitals need to increase the degree to which they specify a 'concern for shareholders/funders' in their mission.

On the other hand, the low frequency of mentioning shareholders/funders may simply be due to faith-based modesty: the hospital founders, trying to live their own faith-based values, do not ask for or expect personal recognition or satisfaction from the organizations they helped to establish. Thus, expressing a concern for shareholders/funders may be unnecessary because when patients' needs are met in line with the mission (e.g., with dignity, sensitivity, honesty and integrity), the "owners" are automatically satisfied. Hospital managers, therefore, need to be sensitive to the outcome benefits of including shareholders/funders in the mission statement versus the need to respect the values and preferences of the owners.

The Mission Content Satisfaction Nexus

Despite the fact that I found significant differences between faith-based and secular hospitals in the frequency with which certain mission Content items were included, I could find *no* significant difference in terms of respondents' *relatively low* levels of satisfaction with their mission Content. One reason for the low scores may be dissatisfaction with the *mission process* itself, as discussed in Chapter 6. As one respondent from a faith-based hospital wrote on his survey: "If the process is flawed, then how can the final product possibly be perfect?"

Another possibility, however, is that the low satisfaction with mission statement Content may not so much relate to what is included as to what has been excluded. More specifically, faith-based hospitals are traditionally viewed as "values driven" organizations and they have consistently tried to maintain their reputations as *charitable institutions* committed to compassionate care in the community. One might assume that it would be a natural consequence, then, for faith-based hospitals to manifest their concern for *people in general* as widely as possible in their mission statements. Yet, the results of my survey suggest that faith-based hospitals do not extend "compassionate care" to others as much as might be expected. For example: concern for patients was ranked second while concern for employees ranked a distant ninth. Similarly, 'concern for society' (as a distinct and separate stakeholder) was ranked 11th. And perhaps, most interestingly, no significant differences between the two types of hospitals were found for either the employee or society Content items.

One interpretation of the low-frequency Content scores for employees suggests the possibility that hospital staff are being undervalued (or taken for granted) by both faith-based and secular institutions (i.e. "this is what you are expected to do in the job that you get paid to do and so you should not look for anything special from the hospital for doing this"). Another, more plausible one, however, seems to turn, yet again, on the values underlying the organizations in this study. More specifically, there is a belief within many secular and faith-based hospitals (stemming from their founding values) that, given their 'higher purpose' of patient care, employees are expected to suppress their personal and secular needs thereby providing more resources (both emotional and financial) for the patients.

When looking at the historical development of hospitals, one sees not only the founding faith-based orders of "Sisters" and "Brothers" but also such individuals as Florence Nightingale and Clara Barton, all of whom were role models for the self-sacrificing and self-effacing behaviors which were to be encouraged and practiced by all members of the hospital. In Roman Catholicism, for instance, visiting the sick and caring for the dying are considered to be corporal works of mercy expected as a matter of course from all people, not just hospital employees. So, it is not surprising that not only secular, but faith-based hospitals too, omit this important item from their mission statements.

But one of the undesired results of this belief in "higher" values for hospital employees is that altruistic attitudes may be enforced too stringently within the behavior code, both formal and informal. Consequently, staff members may feel themselves to be "wrong" or "selfish" to think of their own needs for secular rewards and/or personal recognition rather than their patients' needs. As "Dr Mark Green" once said in an episode of the highly popular television show "ER": "People come in here sick, bleeding and dying. They need our help and that has to be more important than the way we feel. But, sometimes, that sucks!"

This is not to say that the aspirations and needs of employees are being totally ignored in the mission statements of hospitals in the sample. It's just that the emphasis and priority that "employee needs" appear to be given are patently low and not what they should be. Moreover, the kinds of employee 'needs' or 'concerns' often included as mission Content are not necessarily those which have been shown to be linked to job satisfaction (such as individual and mutual respect; individual recognition for accomplishments (especially praise) and job security), but rather concepts such as openness, honesty, skill development and integrity. These latter items are all laudable areas of employee concern, but they may not be the most important for capturing employees' satisfaction with and commitment to the mission and thereby, ironically, jeopardizing the ability of staff to fulfill its mission of patient care.

Similarly, just as it was for 'concern for employees', the low scores observed for 'concern for society' may also simply be reflective of the overarching emphasis put by both types of hospitals on patient care. But, in so doing, hospitals may actually be missing out on another more subtle way of inspiring and energizing their employees. More specifically, by making themselves highly visible *proactive citizens* in their local communities (as a consequence of expressing a genuine concern for society in their missions), hospitals can confer 'referent recognition' on their employees, making them proud of the institution for which they work and more committed to its values and vision. Thus, I contend that both faith-based and secular institutions appear to be foregoing a powerful inspirational tool when they fail to include 'concern for society' in their mission statements. I also predict that 'satisfaction with mission Content' would probably be higher if both internal stakeholder and societal concerns were included in a hospital's mission statement, thereby giving it a broader appeal and applicability.

To the extent that you think 'employees' and/or 'society' are being neglected in the context of your hospital's mission statement, then, I recommend that you (a) consider ways to better identify employees'/society's needs, (b) revise the mission to raise the profile of employees and society as important stakeholder groups, and (c) specify exactly how their needs are going to be addressed.

WARNING: Do not think that with this new knowledge, you can simply "plop" a sentence or two into your mission statement concerning employees/society to fix this problem. The inclusion of such a concern in a hospital's mission statement must occur naturally as part of the mission development process if it is have the desired impact.

PART 4

Communication—The Faith-based Spin

The Gabriel Factor: Getting The Message Out

In a hospital, the mission-development process is a kind of intelligence-gathering exercise: the more stakeholders contacted and listened to, the more genuine and accurate the "message" developed in the mission statement. However, simply developing a hospital's mission statement, no matter how brilliantly written it is, is insufficient without Communicating it effectively to all appropriate parties. As discussed in Chapter 6, it is 'best practice' to Communicate the mission to all key hospital stakeholder groups, but primarily the internal ones, using as many types of media as possible. It is absolutely crucial that those responsible for implementing and delivering the mission to patients (i.e. the internal stakeholder employees) *know, understand, accept and remember the mission.* Yet, it is also important for external stakeholders to receive the mission message for two key reasons:

- Potential patients can be drawn to a particular hospital because of its "advertised" concern for their needs; and
- Informing patients (or potential ones) deliberately, explicitly and regularly about a hospital's mission will raise their level of awareness about how they might expect to be treated.

Both of these factors, in turn, influence the behavior of hospital employees by making them much more sensitive to patients whose expectations have been knowingly increased and who might now analyze and evaluate the quality of care that they are receiving much more critically. Informing patients about the hospital's mission also contributes to employee satisfaction with the mission because it shows hospital employees that the mission is real and that the hospital is taking the mission seriously. Thus, informing patients about the mission is an indirect method for influencing the behavior of hospital employees—*the ultimate target of mission statements.*

When it comes to Communicating a hospital's mission to various stakeholder groups, I found that there were essentially no differences between secular and faith-based hospitals. There were also no differences noted between them in the effectiveness of their Communications (with one exception discussed below).

What do these results indicate? In the first place, it appears that both secular and faith-based hospitals are trying to Communicate their mission message as widely as possible—and this is a good thing. But, just because a mission statement has been Communicated is no guarantee that it has been done so effectively (i.e. that the mission message has been received, understood and remembered). As discussed in Chapter 6, the more a mission statement is *Communicated well* to stakeholder groups, the greater the satisfaction with the mission Content, the mission process and other performance outcomes associated with being mission-driven.

Unfortunately, I observed that the 'level of mission Communication effectiveness' appeared to be a major problem for all of the hospitals in our sample. More specifically, I found for each type of hospital: that there were wide differences in the quality with which the mission statement was Communicated to different stakeholder groups; that the effectiveness of Communication decreased with the internal stakeholders' level (and even more so with patients); and that, astonishingly, there was not one stakeholder group to whom the mission statement was Communicated with 100 percent effectiveness—including the CEO and senior management.

These results, therefore, help explain some of the performance outcomes that I observed. In particular, when it comes to disseminating a hospital's mission, it appears that both faith-based and secular hospitals are equally *mal adroit*. They both appear to be equally unknowledgeable of the simple truth that if a mission statement is not well understood or accepted, no one will be satisfied with it. And if no one knows or understands it thoroughly enough, no one can really take direction from it. Consequently, it was no wonder that only relatively modest levels of satisfaction were obtained for the mission statements in this study and that mission statements were often not used for decision-making purposes in any of our hospitals.

To be sure, the words contained in a mission statement may (from an emotional perspective) promote certain feelings and behaviors because of their sound, tone and cadence. My findings, however, suggest that hospital managers may to be depriving their institutions from the full benefit of their employees' intellectual capital, decision making efficacy and personal energy when there is uncertainty, ambiguity and confusion concerning the meaning, interpretation and translation of all the "nice sounding words". Hospital administrators of both faith-based and secular institutions (as well as their senior managers), thus, need to put much more effort into ensuring that the mission message is not just Communicated—but, Communicated extremely well.

Interestingly, my comparative analysis also revealed that there was one stakeholder group with which faith-based hospitals managed to communicate significantly better than their secular counterparts— their shareholders/funders. One explanation for this finding is that the faith-based hospitals' affiliation with powerful faith-based institutions and religious orders produces a "more active and more concerned shareholder/owner". Another is that managers of faith-based hospitals may simply feel more compelled to relate and explain their organization's mission when reporting to individuals who bear such titles as "Reverend Mother", "Monsignor", "Bishop" and "Your Excellency".

Nevertheless, faith-based institutions should take little comfort and solace in their apparent advantage over their secular counterparts on this item since, *at the rank of sixth*, "faith-based shareholders" was still one of the stakeholders to whom the mission statement was Communicated least effectively. Hospital administrators of both secular and faith-based hospitals would, therefore, do well to consider placing greater emphasis in disseminating their mission more effectively to all stakeholders groups in order to maximize their mission's impact.

Communication Methods—The Medium is the Message

Chapter 6 noted that the way in which the mission message is Communicated, *principally the volume and choice of methods*, contributes to its effective assimilation by the organization. Specifically,

I showed that the more methods the hospitals used to Communicate their mission, the greater was the impact on performance. However, not all Communication methods proved to be equally effective and that the highest, most far-reaching performance impact was found in the use of posters and word-of-mouth (or person-to-person) explanations.

In my comparison of faith-based and secular hospitals, I noticed that some Communication methods, especially the printed ones, were used to a fairly high degree by both types. Moreover, only in the case of "posters", did faith-based hospitals deploy them significantly more than did the seculars. All other methods received low-usage ratings and no others were used significantly more by one type of hospital than the other.

The most likely explanation of these findings is a combination of 'convenience' and 'fear' on the part of hospital administrators. Posters are convenient and definitely cost efficient: they permit easy mass Communication of the mission message at minimum cost. Not only do posters allow for the Communication of complex and abstract ideas/words in a colourful, visual format, they also provide management with the "proof" that the mission has been "officially Communicated."

By using posters to a higher degree, the faith-based hospitals in this study also appear to have benefited more than their secular counter-parts by achieving significantly higher performance scores for 'commitment to mission', 'mission influence over member behaviors' and 'mission as an energy source'. Nevertheless, there is a problem with posters in that while they try to convey an important abstract idea through a picture or drawing, there is no guarantee that all stake-holders will "see" the same image or interpret it in the way management intended.

That's why 'word-of-mouth' Communication of the mission, by which senior managers (or designated others) explain, translate and interpret the mission statement to small groups, is a far more certain and effective way of achieving understanding of and commitment to the mission. Word of mouth, though, can be extremely slow, time-consuming and expensive; it can also be a frightening experience for senior executives who are themselves unsure and uncertain about what the mission means. As a result, senior managers will often choose to hide under the cover of "official" written Communications rather than use team-building, small-group discussions of the mission in which the Leader might say: "I am not completely sure what these words mean right now for any of us, but together we will give them meaning and I am counting on each and every one of you to make a contribution to their interpretation." Yet, Communicating the mission orally, through story-telling and personal anecdotes, is perhaps the most powerful way of getting the really important messages contained in the mission across.

Consequently, it is one of the recommendations of this study that hospital administrators need to spend considerably more time explaining, translating and interpreting their mission statements if hospital employees are to get the full benefit of their mission's message. In so doing, hospital employees can finally begin to grasp the subtleties in their mission's words and finesse its implementation. Hospital administrators should also use as many of the Communication methods used in this study as possible (i.e., as is permissible by their budgets) in order to keep the mission's message "remember-able", alive and "front and centre". A high-volume Communication strategy would also aid in the understanding of the mission's message and enhance the effectiveness with which the mission was Communicated.

PART 5

Coordination and Control—Linking Organization with Mission & Performance

As I talked about in Chapter 7, the more a hospital *Coordinates and Controls its mission's implementation through its organizational components* (such as MIS, recruitment, reward and planning/budgeting systems, etc.), the greater the organization's success in becoming *mission-driven*. Indeed, of all the areas which have been cited as important to a hospital's success with its mission, the most significant appears to be the degree of mission-organizational alignment.

This observation makes eminent sense because a hospital's systems and processes represent some of the most direct and explicit influences for creating employee behaviors. When well-Coordinated, a hospital's organizational arrangements inform, educate and direct employees' efforts and attention towards the goals and priorities contained in the hospital's mission. Furthermore, aligning organizational arrangements with mission *focuses* the hospital and gives it a *conviction and cohesion* that can confer tremendous competitive advantage over those institutions that have not similarly used their systems, structures, processes and procedures to Coordinate and Control their mission's implementation.

Interestingly, I discovered that **all the hospitals in my study appeared to Coordinate and Control their mission with mixed intensity and wide variability.** In particular, I observed that some organizational components (which were almost entirely Coordination mechanisms) were very well aligned with a hospital's mission while others (which were almost entirely Control mechanisms) were not. Moreover, none of the hospitals' various organizational arrangements was found to be matched *completely* to their mission in all circumstances.

Consequently, the alignment results I observed add further to our understanding of the performance outcomes: they suggest that the organizational components in both faith-based and secular hospitals did not sufficiently support their missions and hence may be responsible for not achieving higher levels of mission-driven performance.

I believe that the most likely explanation for these findings is that large numbers of faith-based and secular administrators simply do not understand the *highly significant* role (that we have now discovered) organizational alignment plays in driving "mission performance". Additionally, many senior managers' attitudes concerning mission statements are highly jaundiced from bad experiences with trying to implement them in previous jobs or careers. So it is important to spread the "good news" about mission statements coming from this study: *that increasing the degree of a hospital's mission-organizational alignment will go far to increasing its performance and its ability to become mission-driven.*

Mission Alignment and Performance: The Faith-based Style

Thus far I have discussed the hospitals' rather "tepid" mission-organizational alignment and performance outcomes. But there is still a number of major differences between faith-based and secular hospitals on these matters worth pointing out, namely:

- faith-based hospitals achieved significantly higher levels of mission-organizational alignment for 'job descriptions', 'types of rewards' and 'the promotion system'; and
- faith-based hospitals had significantly greater performance outcomes on such items as 'achievement of the mission', 'mission as a source of energy', 'commitment to the mission' and 'influence over organization members'.

It seems fair to assume that the significant differences in performance for the faith-based hospitals can be attributed at least in part to their better mission-organizational alignment. I contend that, because of these three areas of organizational differentiation, employees in faith-based hospitals have a better understanding of what behaviors are expected of them and what actions are sanctioned, encouraged and rewarded for achieving the mission than in secular hospitals. In essence, these are the critical Coordination and Control mechanisms in the 5-C Mission Model and the results of their significant (and combined) mission-organizational alignment can be seen in the greater commitment to mission amongst the faith-based hospitals.

But why not go all the way?

At first glance, the findings and observations on Coordination and Control appear to provide concrete evidence that faith-based hospitals do indeed do it better: By better aligning some of their organizational arrangements with mission, they appear to receive some higher performance outcomes. They are more mission-driven. And this is true. But, this also takes the findings just discussed purely at face value.

Looking more closely at the survey results, I found that the observed performance levels for both faith-based and secular hospitals were generally quite low and the *absolute* differences between them not always great. Thus, to increase performance outcomes, both types of hospitals need to increase the degree to which they Coordinate and Control their mission i.e. they need especially to **increase their mission-organizational alignment overall.**

And, as I noted in Chapter 7, it is also important to **increase the degree of organizational alignment for each component** in tandem so as to increase the degree of **congruence** among them (i.e. the degree to which each organizational component supports and works in harmony with the others). This creates a powerful association—as well as a **synergy**—with performance.

Yet, many of the hospitals in this study did not appear to grasp this dynamic.

For example, neither faith-based nor secular hospitals appear to generally recruit employees based on (or in reference to) their stated mission. What happens consequently is that hospitals find themselves hiring employees with diverse *values* that may conflict with those of the organization, such as pro-choice-ers in a right-to-life environment. Faith-based hospitals appear to deal with this issue by creating a "put-up and shut-up atmosphere" in which organizational values are stressed and enforced through the reward and promotion systems. Or, as one Chief of Staff from a faith-based hospital—who confessed to being an agnostic—told me: "If you want to get ahead here, you'd better play the game by *their* rules." On the other hand, the secular hospitals seem to simply ignore the issue altogether.

Avoiding the issue of who-to-recruit, however, undermines the possibility of creating passionate commitment to organizational values that might occur from using the mission as a screening mechanism when hiring. This does not mean that faith-based hospitals would only hire those individuals who were part of their church community—in other words, discriminating by faith-based persuasion. Rather, the "discrimination" in hiring would depend on the values embodied in the mission that resonate deeply within the psyches of people from many different faiths and philosophies. **Hence, both faith-based and secular hospitals could strengthen their organizational commitment to mission by aligning recruitment policy with it.**

As with recruitment, training and development for hospital staff could be a powerful tool for building 'mission commitment' and directing behavioral change in line with a hospital's mission. I found, though, that for both faith-based and secular hospitals, the degree of mission-organizational alignment on this dimension was fairly low. Common sense suggests that by using a hospital's mission as a template for the selection of training topics for hospital staff (e.g., patient satisfaction, team building, Communicating openly, etc.), the mission has a greater probability of affecting employee behavior, influencing their day-to-day actions and guiding resource allocations in the short and long term. This should also raise the level of the performance outcomes used in this study to a more acceptable level. In short, they will become *more* mission-driven!

Even worse: Working at cross-purposes!

Interestingly, after a still closer look, I observed that, in *both types of hospitals,* the failure of some organizational systems to support or reinforce each other sufficiently in their alignment with the mission actually caused them to work at cross purposes with one another! For example, while strategic plans and objectives were observed to be moderately aligned with the mission, budgets, performance evaluation criteria and management information systems (all areas crucial for achieving high mission performance) were relatively low in alignment. As a result of this, *the strategic plans and objectives that ultimately enhance a mission's interpretation and execution **were not being sufficiently translated** into specific resource allocations—either through a budget or by an individual hospital manager's objectives.* This can naturally lead to dysfunctional, irrational behaviors which in turn put the organization into conflict and at risk. I contend that it is this incongruence between mission Coordination and Control mechanisms that helps partially explain and contribute to the low satisfaction levels reported with the various hospitals' mission statements.

It is also very disturbing that management information and performance reporting systems (MIS) received the lowest alignment rating of all for faith-based hospitals and the second lowest for seculars. This is strange behavior when compared to our earlier observation that hospitals worked fairly hard at aligning their strategic plans and objectives with their missions. It especially makes evaluation of the progress of a mission's implementation almost impossible since it is a hospital's management information system which would provide the measures and reporting mechanisms critical to charting the mission's accomplishment. Moreover, this incongruity hampers the hospital leaders' ability to correct or adjust their mission routinely since, as the old adage says: "You can't manage what you don't measure."

DUE TO THESE OBSERVATIONS, I have concluded that the hospitals in my sample—both secular and faith-based—did not work diligently enough to carry out their missions thoroughly and that they failed to establish the necessary Coordination and Control to get the maximum performance results and become *completely mission-driven*. Without this strong mission-organization alignment, hospitals are forced to rely much more on employees' good will—and the power of the mission message itself—to inspire them to the desired behaviors. But as I have shown throughout this discussion, the way in which hospitals undertake the first three C's of mission are, in fact, typically flawed. Hence, higher levels of mission-organizational alignment are the only method left to compensate for these problems and to drive higher mission performance outcomes.

Given their interest in values, motivation and behaviors, faith-based hospital managers should be well attuned to this mission-organizational-alignment message but it is not for them alone. Indeed, I propose that hospitals of all types need to revamp their approach to mission-organizational alignment so as to obtain the maximum performance results from their mission. **All hospital administrators,** not just those in faith-based hospitals, **need to align as many of their key organizational systems and procedures as possible to their mission and *as much* as possible.** Those hospitals that heed this message, I predict, will be catapulted to the head of the performance race and be well on their way to becoming *mission-driven*.

PART 6

Some Final, Final Thoughts

At the beginning of this chapter I announced my desire to try to see whether faith-based hospitals "do it" better than secular ones when it comes to 'making mission' and making it matter more. Along the way, I found that there are indeed some significant differences between them which relate to each aspect of the **5-C Mission Model** and various mission performance outcomes. Significantly, all of these differences were always observed to be at a higher level in faith-based hospitals than the secular ones.

Faith-based institutions, therefore, appeared to be more mission-driven. However, a nagging problem was that the overall performance results achieved by both types of hospitals were not that high. In all, then, while faith-based hospitals did marginally do "it" better, the overall performance results for both types of hospitals was disappointing.

Considering the enormous demands and stress being placed on all healthcare institutions worldwide, it is surprising that the power of the mission statement—*as executed through a mission-driven organization*—is not being utilized to its utmost. Hopefully, armed with the lessons learned in this study, hospital administrators everywhere (as well as their Boards) will have new insights and ways that they can improve their mission outcomes and, in so doing, **create strong, viable and fiscally sustainable healthcare organizations.**

The end.

Please visit http://MissionDrivenHospital.com

Dr. Chris Bart, FCPA

DR. CHRIS BART is the world's leading authority on organizational mission and vision statements. He is the
**Founder, Principal and Lead Professor
of the Directors College** at McMaster
University, Canada's first university
accredited corporate director certifi-
cation program. He is also the **founding CEO** of **Corporate Missions Inc.**,
a unique consulting firm dedicated to
helping organizations both develop
better mission (and vision) statements
and overcome the #1 cause of their
failure: poor execution. In 2003, Dr. Bart authored *"A Tale of Two
Employees and the Person Who Wanted to lead Them"*—which has
been on the Canadian business books Best Sellers list for the past 10
years—and he has recently published the third edition of his widely
acclaimed monograph, *"20 Essential Questions Corporate Directors
Should Ask About Strategy (2013)"* as well as co-authored the much
anticipated *"Achieving the execution edge: 20 Essential Questions
Corporate Directors Need to Get Answered about Strategy Execution
(2013)"*.

Through his pioneering research and teachings, Dr. Bart has
become highly sought after by organizations seeking to develop
vision and mission statements that get results. His practical approach
for bringing mission statements to life has inspired business leaders
and audiences around the world.

As a **Professor of Strategy and Governance** at McMaster University's DeGroote School of Business, Dr. Bart has published over 170 articles, cases and reviews. He currently serves as **Associate Editor** of the **International Journal of Business Governance & Ethics**. He is also an **innovator.** He helped establish the Management of Innovation and New Technology Research Centre (MINT~RC) at McMaster and was its first Director. Later, he devised and created the Innovation Management Network; a worldwide association of academics and practitioners who collaborate through the internet on matters of innovation and new technology.

Dr. Bart has been awarded the **Ontario Chamber of Commerce** "Outstanding Business Achievement Award for Corporate Governance", the **Hamilton Chamber of Commerce** "HR Hero Award", the **United Way** "Chairman's Award", the HRPA 2011 "Summit Award for Corporate Governance & Strategic Leadership", and McMaster's "Innovation Award". In 2012, Dr. Bart was the recipient of the **Queen Elizabeth II Diamond Jubilee Medal** for service to Canada. For his research, he has received both the McMaster **Research Recognition Award** and its **Theory to Practice Award.**

A highly regarded lecturer, Dr. Bart has received both the "Outstanding Undergraduate Business Professor" and "MBA Professor of the Year" awards on multiple occasions. He has also won "**The President's Award for Teaching Excellence**", McMaster's highest teaching award—which made him the most decorated professor at the DeGroote School. In 2009, his CPA designation was elevated to **FCPA** (Fellow of the Institute of Chartered Professional Accountants).

Over the years, Dr. Bart has been invited to lecture at numerous institutions throughout the world, including South Africa, Switzerland, the United Kingdom, Australia, the Czech Republic and China.

Dr. Bart is listed in **Canadian Who's Who** and has been a director on many boards.

Contact Information:
Dr. Chris Bart, FCPA
chrisbart@corporatemissionsinc.com,
(905)-515-6399
www.corporatemissionsinc.com

Some of the other publications
by Dr. Chris Bart, FCA

A Tale of Two Employees and the person who wanted to lead them.
Sex, lies and mission statements
Developing Mission Statements which Work
Industrial Firms and the Power of Mission
The Impact of Mission on Firm Innovativeness
Mission Possible
Mission Matters
Making Mission Statements Count
Accepting the Mission
Lasting Inspiration
Who's Running the Store?
The Relationship Between Mission Statements and Firm Performance:
    An Exploratory Study
Exploring the Application of Mission Statements on the Internet
Measuring the mission effect in human intellectual capital
Innovation, Mission Statements and Learning
A Comparison of Mission Statements and their Rationales in Innovative
    and Non-Innovative Firms
Distinguishing Between the Board and Management in Company
    Mission: Implications for Corporate Governance
Mission statements in Canadian Hospitals

Mission Statement Content and Hospital Performance in the Canadian Not-for-Profit Healthcare Sector

Mission Statement Rationales and Organizational Alignment in the Not-for-profit Healthcare Sector

Mission Statements in Canadian Not-for-Profit Hospitals: Does Process Mattter?

A Model of the Impact of Mission Rationale, Content, Process and Alignment on Firm Performance

The governance role of the board in strategy: An initial progress report

The Governance Role of the Board in Corporate Strategy: A Comparison of Board Practices in 'For Profit' and 'Not-for-profit' Organizations

An Empirical Examination of the Content and Composition of Board Charters Issues in Canadian Board Transparency

A comparative analysis of mission statement content in secular and faith based hospitals

High-Tech Firms: Does Mission Matter

Mission Use and Innovation in the Airline Industry: An Exploratory Investigation

Improving the board's involvement in corporate strategy: Directors speak out

Leveraging Human Intellectual capital through an Employee Volunteer Program and Service-Learning: The Case of Ford Motor Company of Canada

The Role of the Board in IT Governance: Current and Desired Oversight Practices

A Tale of Two Employees and the person who wanted to lead them.